APOCALYPSE NO

Also by Michael Adzema

From the Return to Grace series

Culture War, Class War. Volume 1
Apocalypse Emergency. Volume 3
Experience Is Divinity. Volume 8

Wounded Deer and Centaurs. Volume 5 (forthcoming)
The Great Reveal by the Planetmates. Volume 6 (forthcoming)
Funny God. Volume 7 (forthcoming)
Falls from Grace. Volume 9 (forthcoming)
Primal Return. Volume 10 (forthcoming)

APOCALYPSE NO

Apocalypse or Earth Rebirth and the Emerging Perinatal Unconscious

Return to Grace, Volume 4

MICHAEL ADZEMA

I dedicate this book to all life on planet Earth ... to all planetmates, human and otherwise

CONTENTS

	Acknowledgments	xi
PART 1	THE PERINATAL UNCONSCIOUS	
Chapter 1	Strange Days	1
Chapter 2	"We Ain't Born Typical"	11
Chapter 3	The Perinatal Media	17
Chapter 4	Twenty-First Century and Its Discontents	43
Chapter 5	Birth Wars, World Woes	59
PART 2	WHAT IT IS THAT IS HAPPENING HERE	
Chapter 6	Healing Crisis — Getting "Sick" to Be Well	69
Chapter 7	Through Gaia's Eyes — Nature Balances HerSelf	96
PART 3	APOCALYPSE OR EARTH REBIRTH	
Chapter 8	Derailing the Cycles of War and Violence	115
Chapter 9	Regressions in the Service of Society — Messy Healing	134
Chapter 10	Where There Is Hope, Cultural Rebirthing	153
Chapter 11	Control Versus Surrender ... Heaven Leads Through Hell	168
Chapter 12	Atman Projects Versus Surrender Solutions	178

Chapter 13   Peaceful Warriors and Silly Heroes   187

Chapter 14   To Move the World — A Race Against Time   195

Afterword   Centaurs, Shamans, Sacrificial Lambs, and Scapegoats: 201
              Reflections on a Collective Shadow and Experience as
              Primary

              Notes   209

              About the Author   233

ACKNOWLEDGMENTS

I am ever grateful for the invaluable support and constant love of my wife, Mary Lynn Adzema. Truly we have shared our thoughts and feelings in the creation and inspiration of everything I write. Who but the most stalwart and worthy, or mad, would travel with this mind of mine?

I need to thank Carl Jung, Hermann Hesse, Arthur Janov, Stanislav Grof, Lloyd deMause, and Sathya Sai Baba for their profound inspiration to myself in life and in particular in the creation of this work.

I wish to mention Meyer Tope, Albert Sallitt, Richard French, and Sharon Coggan — teachers from long ago. You have no idea how you have affected my life.

I owe much to Warren A. Baker, M.D., Jules Roth, and Helen Roth, for making available and guiding me on the path of primal therapy, which has transformed and infused my life immeasurably.

In the actual production of this book, I want to mention Mary Lynn Adzema's help in editing and as sound board on ideas, Peter Radford's and Atilla Vijada's input on cover design, Debbie Condon's feedback and support, and Ceila Starshine Levine's input and support overall. Thanks are due all the people I will never meet in person on the internet and especially Facebook who have had a say on every aspect of this book — contents to cover. The feedback and comments from, literally, thousands of minds over the last two and a half years has clearly identified to me its audience and have elevated this work above what it would have been..

Finally, I want to thank my mother, Margaret Adzema, and my father, Joseph Adzema, for their right-handed and left-handed help in making me what I am. I will be ever grateful to my grandmother, Mary Derzak, for embodying love, my grandfather, Andrew Derzak, for modeling humor and kindness, and my aunt, Martha Ello, for always being in my corner. I wish to acknowledge my brothers and sisters — Joseph Adams, Mary Ann Lewis, Chuckie Adzema, Peggy Pritchard, and James Adzema — for being there in good times and bad, but most of all for providing me with that bottom-most sense of belonging, the solidarity of my first "union" ... the knowing both that we are all in this together as well as that whatever I do I do for us all.

PART ONE

THE PERINATAL UNCONSCIOUS

CHAPTER 1

STRANGE DAYS

Something's Happening Here

"Nobody Told Me There'd Be Days Like These" — John Lennon

We live in unprecedented times — times in which the possibility of ending our species in our lifetime, even eliminating all life on this planet, are very real possibilities. No other time has been like this. And the effect of this possibility of the actual end of days, so to speak — while so horrifying that we are in denial of it and hardly speak it — hangs over us and affects us in ways unique and fantastic.

We will either heroically, somehow, save our species and our planet, which will require a change of our human nature unlike anything that has been asked of our species ever before, or we will be witnesses to the elimination of life on this planet in some way that we cannot imagine but can only be horrific in the extreme.

This book is about facing, not denying, the uniquely dire character of our times and finding out what it says about us and requires of us. But it is also about what it is about our species that we — of all the other species here — are the ones, the only ones, who would bring about such a possibility.

Why Do We Poop Where We Sleep?

Just what is it about us that could allow us to so violate our home as to make the death of us all possible? This is something that somebody should be addressing, don't you think? I will begin that here. Come along, if you dare.

But this is not for those who would prefer to keep their heads in the sand and to sleepwalk through life. Certainly that is part of the reason we could get to this pass. But it is doubtful that such people, in such deep denial of the signs around them, would be able to hear what is here being brought to light. If instead you are of the type that would wish to look fiercely at the truth, no matter how horrifying it might be, and to truly witness and be awake in these most fantastic of times, then listen up.

Gaia's Calling You.

There is much here to see, and so much of it the mainstream would never touch for fear of creating a panic. Still, to survive our species must face our problems, not look away. And there is a nobility in doing that, which is unlike any kind of nobility or heroism that has been asked of our species before. I hope, for the sake of us all, that you are one of those heroes. For we will need many noble souls to reverse our current downslide into oblivion.

"Strange Days, Indeed. Most Peculiar, Mama!" — John Lennon

Something's Happening Here

What it is ain't exactly clear.

"Something's happening here. What it is ain't exactly clear." So goes a hugely popular song from the Sixties by Buffalo Springfield. Meanwhile Jim Morrison of the rock group The Doors sang, "Break on through to the other side."[1]

A decade later John Lennon sang "Strange days, indeed … most peculiar, mama!" That was in the late Seventies; not long afterwards Lennon was murdered. In the Nineties, the group R.E.M. enjoyed enormous success singing, "It's the end of the world, as we know it"; then, singing parenthetically, "and I feel fine."[2]

Break On Through to the Other Side.

My point is that there *is* something happening here … something unprecedented in the entire history of this planet, as far as we are able to know. There are powerful factors and influences at work in our world now that have the capacity to change us and our world in radical ways … for good or ill. My point also is that this unprecedented situation, like the "break on through to the other side" lyric indicates, has something to do with birth feelings, birth trauma — an *emerging perinatal unconscious*.[3]

What I have in mind in the ensuing parts on this topic is to attempt to reawaken you to the unique character of our times. Then I expect to persuade you that this unprecedented era in history is rife with the perinatal, that is, with things having to do with the time around our births.

"We Ain't Born Typical."

This contemporary age is permeated by perinatal symbolism, elements, evidence, behavior, rituals, and situations — in other words, I expect to show that the events of these "strange days" are being sculpted by an emerging perinatal unconscious — an unconscious that was created out of the trauma of our entering into this world, our birth trauma. The Kills, with their release in 2008, enjoyed huge success singing, "You are a fever. You ain't born typical." That's what I'm talking about.[4]

Finally, I intend to say a few words about what might be the outcome of these emerging perinatal trends — Earth rebirth or apocalypse.

Strange Days

For most people, I would assume I am not saying anything new in pointing out that our times are unique. For that matter, all times are unique — unlike any other. But what no other time has seen is the actual — not *imagined* — *possibility*, even *likelihood*, of the "end of the world." That is to say, we are facing the end of our species and maybe all life on this planet along with us. Considering just one scenario, we have the capacity, with only a minuscule amount of our nuclear weapons, to wipe out all life on this planet. We all know this.

"The End Is Nigh!"

I used the phrase, just now, "end of the world," deliberately. For I expect that it will evoke in some a reaction that what I am going to say from here on will be a drawn-out verbal version of a familiar cartoon, depicting a bearded and bedraggled man on a street corner, carrying a sign or wearing a clapboard proclaiming, "The end is near!" and that what I will say will have just about as much credibility as that man's would.

I take that chance to make my first point ... which is: The fact that we can so easily dismiss, ridicule, and smugly deride such ideas of apocalypse points to our complacency with these strangest and most precarious of days. In fact, we have lived with this unprecedented situation — dangling on a thread, as it were, above the abyss of nuclear annihilation, to name just one of the possible forces of extinction ... we've lived with it for so long as for it to seem commonplace — as part of the normal and familiar furniture of our daily lives.

Wtf?

Heads in the Sand

It has become so much a part of our daily lives, in fact, that we hardly give it any thought anymore. But for a moment, let us just imagine a person from a previous time in history being somehow transported into this time and being made to understand the impending forces: environmental collapse, species extinction, nuclear threat, population explosion, virulent epidemic, possibly human-created earthquakes and thus tsunamis, planet poisoning, and so on.

Unless this person was Nostradamus, we can imagine this person would be hugely alarmed, to say the least. This person might well wonder at our nonchalance, or should we say apathy, in the face of such likely, not just potential, apocalypse.[5]

So I will not waste time pointing out the statistics that prove the premise that the current trends we are following are apocalyptic.

We need simply to look to our daily headlines. Need I remind of the dangers from catastrophes like Fukushima and the Gulf Oil Spill?[6]

Care for Some Radiation with that Milk?

We have radiation mixing into the world ecosystem as I write. Fukushima alone is spreading radiation that is off the charts into food, air, oceans, and made it to the East Coast of the U.S. and beyond in just a short time. We also know that nuclear waste needs to be guarded for 25,000 years because of its toxicity ... it is still deadly for 250,000 years. Yet we continue to excrete massive amounts of it into our globe and even after the Fukushima meltdowns to push for building more plants.[7]

Dead Zones and Dolphins

We have watched baby dolphins by the hundreds washing up on Gulf coasts and the creation of hundred mile dead zones in our seas.

BP stupidly used toxic chemicals to disperse the oil rather than to collect it. The dispersants themselves are toxic, but the much bigger crime was to make sure the even more toxic oil — which depletes the oxygen in the water and thus creates the dead zones — would be spread far and wide throughout the global water. Good for BP shares looking like they could fix it, bad for survival of oxygen-breathers on Earth.

So BP's egregiously criminal move was the equivalent of sweeping dirt under the rug to clean up.

Unfortunately there is no "away" in which it can "go." So we have, in this incident alone, precipitated greatly the dying off of the life of the oceans — the oxygen-producing plankton — and, hence, the basis of all life on this planet.

Cough, Cough

To this ravaging of the lungs of the planet add worldwide runaway deforestation, already in full swing. I am practically choking as I think how we then stink up the air with industrial emissions and auto exhausts. Living in the LA area, I can tell you that I feel my mouth is sealed to the end of an exhaust pipe most of the time. So to the dangers bringing on our demise we need to add globally increasing air pollution.

Forget Your Sunscreen, We're All Gonna Fry.

Environmentally also, we have the greenhouse effect — global climate change or warming — the depletion of the ozone layer, and so on.[8]

Al Gore is owed the gratitude of the world informing us of climate change in his book and documentary of the same name, *Inconvenient Truth*.

Meanwhile lots of folks think we have solved the ozone layer problem. We banned fluorocarbons, and we don't hear much about this problem anymore in the media.

Environmental nay-sayers are arguing that we "fixed" this problem, as part of their stance that we need not worry about what we are doing to the planet. But not long ago — April 2011 — CNN broadcast the news that the ozone had been depleted by 40% in the previous two months alone! They immediately turned to an item of dire importance — a snake had gotten loose in New York![9]

Only One Earth, Don't Blow It!

Nor need I elaborate on the nuclear threat — whether precipitated by terrorists, rogue nations, or accident. We know, but do not want to, of the possibility of any one or more of these mad actors employing weapons of mass destruction, possibly leading to ever-mounting rounds of retaliation with eventually no one left standing. Relatedly we push out of our minds the threat of other kinds of weapons — such as biological weapons — getting out of control and creating a worldwide epidemic or holocaust.

Seven Billion and Counting … Now Let's Attack Planned Parenthood! *sarcasm*

Need I mention the continuing explosion of the world's population leading to likely famine, wars, diseases, and so on? We have twice as many people alive now as the *combined total* of all humans who have *ever* lived! We are no different from bacteria who overrun their petri dish only to die off. We certainly aren't showing ourselves to be any smarter than that.[10]

Outbreak

How about the possibility of virulent epidemic that cannot be cured? Does that catch your fancy? Strains of micro-organisms are evolving that are immune to our much-touted antibiotics.

You Sure You Should Be Reading This?

What Island Were You Stranded On?

But why go on? If you are not aware of these things, you are from some other planet. If you are dismissing these facts, you are in actual psychological denial of your dire situation. If you are not paying attention, you are spending your life desperately running away.

No, I will not go into stats and figures to support the premise. The evidence and statistics are there for all to see, crying for attention, put out, published, and promulgated by the best scientists of our time, mixed in with the more mundane messages of our daily newspapers and nightly newscasts, though we mostly turn our ears from them.

We'll Try to Save You, Too.

In fact, if you are not already aware of the global crisis that besets us, I do not think you will get much out of reading further in this book and would probably better spend your time doing something else. There will always be those that will have their heads in the sand and will be cast about like flotsam upon the waters by the events swirling around them — impotent in the face of them and dependent upon other's actions for the result. If you are one, know we're trying to save you, too.

Assuming you are not one of them — a good bet, if you have managed to get to this paragraph — there is much to say about the current apocalyptic trends.

Facing Foursquare

But even those of us aware of this crisis hardly think of it. Of course it is our normal psychic defenses that operate to keep this huge awareness out of our daily minds; we *must* do this in order to be able to function. But perhaps, for some of us, our defenses work too well — so much so that we unthinkingly participate in and contribute to our own demise. This is classic neurotic self-sabotaging, self-destruction on a macro scale.

However, psychologists, historians, psychohistorians, and scholars and the educated public claim not to be like that. It is their job, or their claim, to be looking squarely into the face of these forces of denial and potential apocalypse and to be seeking to understand the human condition and human psychology in light of them. It is their duty then to inform the rest of us about what they see so that we might have a chance of reversing our self-destructive tendencies.

If You're Not Alarmed, You're Not Paying Attention.

Whether the educated public and the multitude of scholars actually are fulfilling their mission in these times is debatable.

Regardless, my thesis is that *when* we do this, *when* we look foursquare into the face of the global crisis and its accompanying denial, we find that these unprecedented global factors contribute to a unique and unprecedented human condition and psychology. I have seen a bumper sticker around, in California where I live, that proclaims, "If you're not angry, you're not paying attention!" It could as easily say, however, "If you're not alarmed," fearful, anxious, depressed . . . you name it, *"You're not* paying attention!"

To Face These Maddest of Days and Minds

So then let us pay attention. This book is about facing foursquare into the fantastic circumstances and situation in which we find ourselves, watching, like a photograph emerging in solution, as the face of these times slowly comes into view, and then waking up to the meaning of the message, perhaps the warning, it brings us, so that we might live most fully and take up our roles consciously amid these unprecedented unfoldings. What is required of us now, then, having turned to receive the message, is to look deep into the features of our age. Let us begin.

CHAPTER 2

"WE AIN'T BORN TYPICAL"

"Perinatal" = "Surrounding Birth"

"We Are a Fever"

How are we to characterize these strangest of days and the current unprecedented global condition? As I have said, they are driven by what I call an *emerging perinatal unconscious*. As The Kills sang it, most aptly, "We ain't born typical."[1]

Perinatal Unconscious

Why *perinatal*? First, let us remind ourselves that *perinatal* means, literally, "surrounding birth." As a one-time university instructor of pre- and perinatal psychology and as an editor of a professional journal concerned with perinatal psychology — as well as a psychohistorian, let me explain what might be considered elements of a *perinatal unconscious*.[2]

Unconscious Matrices = "Human Nature"

The elements I will describe are near universally accepted among perinatal psychologists as unconscious forces, factors, matrices that exist in us all as a result of a human birth that is unique, by comparison to *all* other species, in its degree of trauma and hence of its impact or imprint on what we might call — dare I say the word — our "human nature."

These perinatal elements have come to our understanding through the efforts of both the inner explorations of experiential pioneers into the perinatal, as well as the hard empirical work of pre- and perinatal researchers. I might also point out that I, myself, have over forty years of experiential exploration into these perinatal elements, in addition to my scholarly work and research in this field. My experiences confirm, in my own mind, their absolute validity, as well as validating for myself the theoretical constructs put forth by others to describe and explain them.

Pre- and Perinatal Psychology, Experiential Voyagers

Be that as it may, these perinatal elements in the unconscious have been described most thoroughly by three figures in particular: Stanislav Grof, Arthur Janov, and Lloyd deMause. It might help, also, to keep in mind that entire new fields of pre- and perinatal psychology, primal psychology, and to some extent, transpersonal psychology have grown up around the existence of these perinatal factors. Entire modalities of healing tap in to and are based on the existence of this perinatal unconscious, including primal therapy, holotropic breathwork, and rebirthing, to name just the few that I happen to be trained in. These unconscious perinatal elements have, at this point, been confirmed by thousands of researchers and hundreds of thousands, if not millions, of experiential voyagers into the perinatal unconscious.

Elements of Birth Experience

Based upon all this, then, let us look at some of the elements, in general, that characterize this perinatal unconscious.

Perinatal Matrix ~ Societal Matrix

Stanislav Grof describes *basic perinatal matrices (BPMs)* — in other words, typical experiential constellations related to our births. These happen to be very much akin to deMause's perinatal schema, with some slight differences in emphasis, and more elaboration on the part of Grof. So let us use Grof's schema as a basis.[3]

All Needs Met . . . With Luck — Matrix 1

Grof's *Basic Perinatal Matrix I*, or *BPM I*, involves the experiences and feelings related to the sometimes, or at least relatively, undisturbed prenatal period. The prenatal period is that time in the womb sometimes characterized by feelings of peace, complete relaxation, and a feeling of all needs met, or "oceanic bliss."

BPM I corresponds to deMause's societal periods of "prosperity and progress," which he claims are accompanied by feelings and fears of being "soft" and "feminine" — understandably here, for in BPM I, that is, prenatally, the fetus is largely identified with his or her mother and is very much "soft," that is to say, undefended.

The time in the womb may also be disturbed by toxic substances that the mother ingests — drugs, chemical additives, and so on — as well as by disturbing emotions that the mother experiences, which release stress hormones into the mother's bloodstream, which then cross the placental barrier and affect the fetus. For these reasons, BPM I is also sometimes characterized as feelings of being surrounded by a polluted environment and being forced to ingest noxious substances, toxins, and poisons, which sicken the fetus.

No-Exit Despair — Matrix 2

In Grof's schema, BPM I is followed by *BPM II* — that is, *Basic Perinatal Matrix II* — which are experiences and feelings related to the time of "no exit" in the womb and claustrophobic-like feelings occurring to nearly all humans in the late stages of pregnancy and especially with the onset of labor, when the cervix is not yet dilated. Since there does not seem to be any "light at the end of the tunnel" — metaphorically speaking — it is characterized by feelings of depression, guilt, despair, and blame, and a characterization of oneself as being in the position of "the victim."

It is very much like deMause's period of collective feelings of entrapment, strangulation, suffocation, and poisonous placenta, which he has found to precede the actual outbreak of war or other violence.[4]

Birth Wars — Matrix 3

This of course is followed by *BPM III* (*Basic Perinatal Matrix III*), which involves feelings and experiences of all-encompassing struggle and is related to the time of one's actual birth. Characterized also by intense feelings of aggression and sexual excess — in the position, now, of "the aggressor" — it is related directly, in deMause's schema, to a time of actual war.

Hallelujah! . . (I think. . . .) — Matrix 4

Basic Perinatal Matrix IV (*BPM IV*) follows this; it corresponds to the time of emergence from the womb during the birth process and is characterized by feelings of victory, release, exultation.

But also sometimes, after that initial relief, it is followed by depression — when the struggle does not bring the expected rewards, as when, during modern obstetrical births, the neonate is harshly treated and then taken away from the mother, disallowing the bonding which should occur, naturally, immediately after birth.

In my own experience, the exultation and relief of release was replaced suddenly by feelings of being assaulted by the attendants at my birth ... which of course they thought of as "attending" to me ... as they went about roughly removing mucous from my mouth; prematurely cutting my umbilical cord to leave me struggling for breath; scrubbing, weighing, measuring, and otherwise probing me; and wrapping me like a tamale and taking me away from all I had previously known ... that is to say, my mother. This felt like ritual abuse to me, and I have often likened it, after the intense period of compression and crushing before birth, to a situation of "going from the frying pan into the fire."

At any rate, this experience of actual emergence or birth coincides, societally, with deMause's period of the ending of a war.

Heaven and Hell

In summary, we have euphoric, oceanic, blissful feelings, sometimes feelings of being poisoned or being in a toxic or polluted environment; followed by crushing, no-exit, depression, claustrophobia, compression, strangulation, suffocation, and being force-fed by a poisonous placenta; followed by struggle, violence, war scenarios, birth/death fantasies, sexual excess; and finally release, triumph, feeling of renewal or rebirth and a new golden age, but also possibly of being abandoned, tortured, ritually sacrificed, probed medically, and assaulted by sensations. These are some of the elements that characterize the experience of the perinatal unconscious.

For Dreaming Out Loud! Projecting the Perinatal Zeitgeist

In the next chapter, "The Perinatal Media," we will take a look at how these elements have erupted into our collective dreams in recent history. By this I mean, we will see how our artists and creative people have projected them into the media, movies, and TV — in which we all participate — and how our fascination with them, because these artists are reflecting things that exist deep inside of ourselves as well, has caused them to grow, creating the dominant underlying zeitgeist of our time.

CHAPTER 3

THE PERINATAL MEDIA

With these elements of birth experience in mind, let us look at some of the forces and elements, unprecedented and otherwise, that characterize our times.

Baby and Fetal Projections on the Silver Screen

Fetus in the Sky with Diamonds ... And Oh, the Shark Has Pretty Teeth, Dear ...

In these strange days, movies, TV shows, and books are rife with perinatal themes: From the famous ending image of the movie *2001*, where the fetus is pictured against the blackness of space as a newborn star ... to some of the most popular and lucrative movies of all time — *Jaws*, for example, with its huge *vagina dentata* shark mouth lurking in the depths of the unconscious (the ocean), signifying the trauma we have around the mother's vagina, the mouth ringed with teeth — the ferocious looking teeth symbolizing the pain and death elements of birth experience.

Other examples of perinatal imagery in the media include those in the movie *Brazil* — the main character being haunted by hordes of infant/fetal faces in particular; *The Abyss*; *Jacob's Ladder*, and *Close Encounters of the Third Kind* — large-headed fetal looking aliens again.

ET, Phone Mom!

Psychodynamic as well as perinatal sequences are displayed in *The Wall* and *Brainstorm*. There is the fascinating womb and fetal symbolism in UFO movies like *Cocoon*; *Cocoon: The Return!*; and *E.T.* — with the fetal-looking alien wanting to "phone home." And of course, we have seen obvious perinatal symbolism in *Independence Day, Fire in the Sky, Jacob's Ladder, Joe Versus the Volcano, Nothing But Trouble*; and in a recurring way on weekly TV series *The X Files, Star Trek, Heroes,* and *The 4400,* among many others.[1]

Avatar is a near perfect depiction of a BPM I state that is interrupted by the later stages of pregnancy and threatened by a mechanized-technological birth. Everything is there as in the womb state: a perfect harmony with Nature … a world tree symbolizing the life-giving placenta … harmony with the Mother, who is the World Mother, a Goddess.

In the Narnia series, the children find a "secret" doorway at the back of a wardrobe (womb symbol) and go from their normal realm into another magical realm. In this — as in many other depictions, such as *Alice in Wonderland, The Matrix,* and *The Wizard of Oz* — we can see both a re-creation of the birth sequence but also the message (from our unconscious selves) that one needs to go back through and re-experience that sequence, as it was left incomplete. This magical realm is thus the womb. And in it lie many of the spiritual truths that we forgot when we came into the world and were overloaded with the pain of birth, which pushed our connection with Nature and the Universe into unconscious memory.

There is a plethora of more recent films rife with perinatal elements: Notable are the Matrix series, *Total Recall*, the Star Wars series, *Dark City*, *The Lathe of Heaven*, the Alien series, *The Tree of Life*, *Ace Ventura: When Nature Calls*, the Batman series, the Hannibal Lector series, *Suckerpunch*, and the Star Trek series. There are too many more to mention.

In addition to its prevalence in science fiction movies, it is replete in the symbolism of horror movies. When you understand this symbolism, you find it saturates the silver screen, popular television, music video and imagery, and the electronic media and arts

Everything You Always Wanted to Know About Being a Baby

Other movies indicating the interest emerging around pre- and perinatal themes are *Look Who's Talking* and *Look Who's Talking Too*, which demonstrate a belief in sperm and egg, womb, and infantile consciousness far beyond what mainstream psychology wants to believe.

Also, there is the hilarious sperm sequence in Woody Allen's *Everything You Always Wanted to Know About Sex* in which he and a slew of others are dressed as individual sperm and dialogue about their upcoming great adventure.

This idea that sperm and ovum have consciousness can also be heard occasionally in comedic monologues on television and elsewhere.

Boob Tube With a View

Speaking of television, there was that very interesting and much heralded episode of the *Moonlighting* series in the late Eighties which — coincidentally employing an article and book title of mine, "A Womb With a View" — showed Bruce Willis in a womb-like enclosure as a fetus viewing, with the help of a higher spiritual ally, the upcoming events of his life. This plot idea was also an amazing, perhaps synchronistic, mirror image of a short story I wrote in 1979 titled "Birthing, Forgetting."[2]

A Hundred Monkeys and Counting

I point out the personal synchronicities because they speak of a "morphic resonance" phenomenon indicating ideas whose time has come. Be that as it may, the episode of *Moonlighting* is further proof of the growing belief in womb consciousness and interest in perinatal events.

Perinatal Faces Poking Out Everywhere

Other perinatal elements that are currently manifesting include:

Satanic Cult Abuse

Reports of Satanic cult abuse graphically depict BPM II perinatal elements. We hear of children and others being immobilized, tied up, and otherwise disempowered. Oftentimes they relate being forced to spend extensive periods of time trapped in tight places and/or symbolically or literally buried under ground.

BPM III elements in cult abuse include the sexual excess/abuse and bloodletting or blood use as in its being poured or used in "anointing."

Cult abuse in film, as well as in real life, especially depict BPM IV elements: Cutting, hurting, torturing, sexually and ritually abusing and "sacrificing" are all very much like an infant's perception/feelings of its experience of its being "attended" to after birth.

The fact that cult rituals often involve a number of other people focusing on an individual who is strapped or held down — the immobilization prior to birth, as well as the helplessness after birth — on something raised, like an altar or table, and then "worked upon" in some way or other is a particularly graphic expression of a neonate's experience of being on a medical table after birth, watched by a number of others and worked on.

The ritualists' use of robes and costumes, especially if they involve covering the face or the wearing of masks, is also not that much different from the way a baby in modern times perceives its welcoming into the world among masked and robed medical personnel.

Serial Rapists and Killers

One can hardly turn on the tube without finding some movie or TV show that is depicting a serial killer or rapist. I do not need to belabor the flooding of news programs with the same kind of material.

But the number of reports relative to victims and harm involved is far less than victims and suffering involved with other horrific events, such as hurricane, earthquake, nuclear radiation, ozone loss, or flood catastrophes, which have less or no perinatal charge about them. This preoccupation with serial violence, torture, and rape indicates BPM III elements of struggle, violence, sexual perversion and excess, as well as the death and torture aspects of being born.

Tube and Cinematic Violence Galore

Simply the amount of violence on television and in movies is a perinatal indicator. These depictions simulate, and stimulate, perinatal feelings in plot elements which are repeated to death.

Matters of Life and Death

We see clichéd regurgitations of being in life and death situations from which one is saved in the "nick of time." This is exactly how it seemed when one was "miraculously" born, suddenly, after what seemed an endless time of suffering in which death was felt to be the only possible outcome.

It's Not the Fourth of July, However … .

You do not seem to be able to see a story that does not have explosions galore.

Such "fireworks" are examples of extreme compression suddenly becoming immense expansiveness and thus symbolize the sudden perinatal change of state from compression inside the womb to previously unknown expansiveness outside the womb as well as the sudden release of tension and compression upon being born.

Explosions also symbolize the immediate assault of sensation upon coming out of the sensorally "muffled" womb.

XXX

There is lots of violence, and of course also sex. Such extreme degrees of sexual explicitness and especially sexual perversity point to strong BPM III influences.

Monsters, Vaginas, and Hairs, Oh My!

Recurring themes of monsters that eat one, for example, *The Alien* movie series, indicate the feelings of fear of death in the mother's womb. This is often portrayed as a huge, threatening mouth surrounded by teeth and, sometimes, hair. This is a symbol found throughout the world. Social scientists refer to it as a *vagina dentata* "mouth."

One most obvious portrayal of this was Steven King's 1995 miniseries, *The Longoliers*. The monsters, shown at the end, turned out to be flying, ball-shaped *vagina dentatas*, complete with hair covering, as in pubic hair. Though Steven King meant this to be frightening, from the perinatal perspective these flying, attacking vaginas are absolutely hilarious.

Time Travel Equals Age Regression

Interestingly, the appearance of the Longoliers is caused by the characters going back in time. Though King has them going back only fifteen minutes, and not age regressing to birth, I thought the fact of time regression was telling in the extreme.

Time travel in general is indicative of the need to go back and fix the trauma of these early events. The Back to the Future series is merely one example. We all know many others.

We have Ever Increasing Cesarean Births

The perinatal roots of these movies are indicated in other ways, for example, the baby alien, in *Alien*, being "born" out of the abdomen.

While a "baby" emerging from a person's midsection is obviously indicative of birth, the fact that it comes bursting out of the belly, rather than the vagina, might also relate to the ever increasing use of cesarean section as a means of birthing in this century.

"Noah, How Long Can You Tread Water?"

Important perinatal influences are evident in the frequency of scenes of death by suffocation, in water or otherwise.

We are immersed in water before birth, placental fluid. Near the end of gestation, the mother, when standing, constricts blood vessels to the fetus. This reduces the blood supply to the fetus and thus less oxygen is received. It is called *fetal malnutrition.* Prior to birth we humans experience suffocation and claustrophobic feelings — we "can't get enough air"! — which seem deadly and unending.

Aw, Hell

The timelessness of prenatal experience at this point — when not getting enough air — feels horrific, an unending nightmare. This part contributes to human ideas of places of forever, endless suffering — for example, hell.

Death by Vegetable

"I Agree, But I don't Like Having It *Shoved Down my Throat*!"

Very interestingly, a more recent addition to this complex has something being forced aggressively down the throat of the victim.

I have noticed an increasing frequency of this version of suffocation in the visual media ever since I first remember seeing it in a scene from the movie *Alien,* where a rolled-up magazine is used as a murder weapon by being forced into the victim's mouth. It seems to be becoming a writer/director's fad, as increasingly creative ways are being imagined to play it out in scripts.

Told You I Didn't Like Vegetables!

Another common variation is when the suffocating item comes *out* of the person's mouth.

In this frequent scenario, the victim is "infected" with some kind of alien spore which grows inside of him or her and comes thrusting up from inside of the person's body and out of the mouth, lodging itself there. Often this alien extrusion looks something like a huge asparagus emerging. This perverse sexual aspect of the image also has roots in perinatal, specifically, BPM III experience.

This "vegetable" eruption always happens suddenly and climactically, and almost always it results in death. Scenes like this I have observed in the movie *Jacob's Ladder*, several times on the hit show *The X Files*, and in many, many other shows.

Gag Me With a Toxin.

This version of suffocation probably has its roots in the force-feeding of toxic elements to the fetus in the womb through the umbilical cord, and is more definitely related — the symbol is probably an amalgamation of both feelings — to the ungentle clearing of fluids from the neonate's mouth by the attendants immediately after birth.

This latter connection — the ungentle mouth cleaning of birth fluids — I can personally validate through my own primal experiences. Apparently I was not alone in being treated this way as a newborn in the 1940s and 1950s in America ... hence its popularity.

Treated Like a "Piece of Meat"

This practice of ungentle mouth clearing — performed by hurried or insensitive, and uninformed, medical personnel, unaware of the consciousness and keen feeling awareness of the neonate — can leave one with lifelong feelings of being treated like a "thing."

Many report having overwhelming feelings of being dealt with mechanically and without respect. It is common for folks to have feelings of "not being seen." People can have lifelong body memories of having one's mouth stretched wide.

These feelings, while they may be reinforced by later life events, oftentimes have roots that go back to a time immediately after birth. At this time, too frequently, the jaw is pulled down for the insertion of fingers and suction devices. It is done in a manner that is excruciatingly painful for a being that has spent his or her entire life — nine months — previous to that in a relatively placid environment with its mouth closed.

This ungentle procedure is also felt as an assault in that it occurs, usually, as the first event a baby is confronted with upon release from the womb. Its tiny mouth — never before fully opened — is often the first focus of attention, as large fingers (relatively) reach in, stretching the previously unopened and unstretched (virgin) mouth ... breaking the metaphorical oral hymen of the neonate in a way that is felt to the infant to be comparable in pattern and violation to oral sexual assault.

Did you ever wonder why so many folks have such terror of seeing a dentist? Did you ever wonder what is the fascination with water-boarding and torture in recent years?

Victims Du Jour

By the way, I might mention that while genuine sexual assault and child sexual abuse is a reality that has long been with us and is only now really coming to light (thankfully), the similarity of this early perinatal experience of ungentle mouth clearing to sexual assault may have something to do with the epidemic of reports of infant sexual abuse that are coming out of counselor's therapy rooms.

Confused interpretations of these reports can happen because most counselors and psychotherapists are ignorant of birth and perinatal trauma and yet more and more of them are allowing bits and pieces of regressive techniques into their standard professional arsenals.

In addition, they throw in these techniques, most often, without qualification or experience with these techniques, and oftentimes out of knowledge gained solely from books or second-handedly ... not to mention rarely, because of professional arrogance, having experienced or undergone these regressions themselves. Combine this inexperienced dredging up of perinatal material with the fact, as I will be continually reiterating throughout this book, that people in these times are closer to their perinatal unconscious, to their birth trauma. One can see how it can easily happen that when feelings of being orally assaulted after birth begin arising within the counseling rooms, they can be interpreted, by therapist or client or both, as early sexual assault — that being the *interpretation du jour*, so to speak, and because, of course, both are ignorant of the fact of birth trauma — its having systematically been resisted and purged from mainstream professional and lay common knowledge, beginning with Freud's rejection of Otto Rank's discovery of it, right down to the present. (But let's not get into that just here.)

Welcome to the World … Now f u

Regardless, the ungentle mouth cleaning is felt not just as a physical assault, it is an outrage to the infant's tender psyche as well — leaving a lifelong and fundamental imprint undergirding and helping to sculpt all later experience — in that it is the first "welcome" to this world. That is to say, the birth struggle ends, there is release … (finally!) … then, "Welcome, baby" — yank! stretch, feel manipulated and used, treated like an object and with no sense that one is a living aware being.

With this in mind — that this "Hello — fuck you!" experience can be the primal (first) experience of this world, of other people, of society — it may be easier to understand the profound fear and anxiety toward other people that resides inside many of us — for example, as in the book title: *I'd Rather Die Than Give a Speech!*

This also sheds light on the seemingly "mindless" violence and rage that is directed back against anonymous people and society in general by certain types of criminals. They can be seen to be acting out their "fuck you" welcome into the world by attacking back and outwardly, rather than this early rage energy being channeled into some of the other, more healing or at least not harmful, responses possible to early assault.

Faces Coming Out of the Walls

I would like to refer to one final perinatal indicator in the visual media, which has been capturing my attention of late … *seeming to be coming out of the very walls at me!* This is — what appears to me to be — a recent and new sort of perinatal symbolism, at least in Western culture.

We have had, over and over again, the image of the "evil fetus" erupting from the abdomen, as in the classic scene from *Alien* as well as that of it emerging from the mouth — as examples, the "volcano-new-species" episode of *The X Files* and the dance hall scene in *Jacob's Ladder* — indicating fetal emergence mixed with ungentle neonatal mouth clearing, as mentioned above.

Membrane Walls

But this new variation of "fetal emergence" has human faces pushing through membrane-like elastic walls!

Ventura Out of the Womb

A good example of this occurs in the movie, *Ace Ventura, Pet Detective, When Nature Calls*. In the Ace Ventura movie, Jim Carrey emerges from inside a mechanical rhino with virtually all birth elements evident.

He is holed up in a hot and suffocating "womb" — that is, he is inside the rhino.

He becomes engaged in a desperate need to get out. Interestingly, the fan — the source of comfort in the rhino (womb) — stops working after a while. This is exactly analogous to the way, when we are fetuses, the nurturing elements of the mother's womb "turn off," in the last stage of gestation, making the womb quite an uncomfortable place indeed.

We see Carrey pushing his face against the elastic, membrane surface of the rhino's posterior in a way graphically suggesting perinatal emergence. The tourists watching this explicitly state that they see it as the rhino giving birth.

We witness the actual "birth": Jim Carrey (Ace Ventura) struggles to make the opening larger and to come out. Finally, he falls, naked wet and curled up fetal- or baby-like, to the ground. The hilarious — and outrageous to the tourists — part is this image of a rhino giving birth to a full-grown naked adult human "baby."

Couldn't Fight Your Way Out of a Plastic Bag!

Other examples of this element of human features pushing through membranes has individuals completely covered and suffocated in membrane-like elastic sheets from which they cannot escape and in which they appear agonized and struggling. A good example of this was in a scene from *Fire In the Sky* that was shown repeatedly on TV to hype the movie when it came out.

Even the invention and use of straitjackets shows our preoccupation with the perinatal, especially as concerns our mental health or well-being. For the message there is that if you "get out of control" you will be put back in a place where you will be forced to comply and will have to learn to deal, as all the rest of us do, with the "existential fact" of needing to conform to the dictates of an overwhelming, dominating, and pervasive other world.

Existential fact is in quotes to point out that this is not an essential fact of existence; rather they seem to be facts to humans because of the experience we share of being in constricting wombs which become uncomfortable and suffocating increasingly near the end. This is an example of what I have termed elsewhere, *biologically constituted realities.*

Of course a similar thing — forcible "re-education" — could be said for the use of jail cells, solitary confinement, and enclosures like "The Hole" during incarceration. Simply the fact that we have a much greater percentage of our population in prisons than any time previously points to our mania of trying to control this aspect of our feelings from our origins ... and of an emerging perinatal unconscious triggering the reaction. In former times, torture devices often employed devices of compression, suffocation, constriction … of the entire body or just the head … and often added the element of prenatal discomfort by adding torture while so enclosed. The Iron "Maiden" is such a device. Note the feminine being employed in the name itself. Could that be any more clear that it is meant to be a painful, tortuous re-creation of being inside one's mother?

Modern movies showing such devices or procedures are indicative of these perinatal elements coming to the surface obviously. One example is *The Man in the Iron Mask*. In a similar respect, I have already mentioned our current preoccupation with water-boarding style torture. In employing suffocation, it is an effective and brutally inhuman way of stimulating people's perinatal pain, just as straitjackets and jail cells are intended to.

This House Will Eat You Alive!

I saw a most potent portrayal of this new perinatal element in a 1990s horror movie.

This movie's plot involved a house being somewhat alive and gobbling people up into the walls. The ingested people would try to emerge from the house's walls. The walls being like elastic when they would do this, the features of their faces could be seen pushing through to the point even of the individuals being identifiable.

These swallowed people could not get out of the walls. And they would be the next ones trying to lure their loved ones and friends into being gobbled up by the house, the same having been done to them, which had resulted in their being taken into the walls initially. Sounds like a modern, very perinatal variation on the Pied Piper theme.

But the former victims who, once pulled into the walls, themselves become perpetrators also is a powerful metaphor of the way primal trauma and child abuse of all kinds — including genital mutilation — is passed from one generation to the next. Vampirism has this telling quality as well: Once you are "bitten," you are compelled to do it to others. In the same way all child abusers were abused themselves as children, as any psychologist will tell you.

House, Cave, Squids

Anyway, this portrayal of a house that gobbles up its victims, bizarre as it sounds and as it looked, can only be explained by looking into our perinatal imprints; and it is rife with such elements.

To start with, a house — being an enclosure in which humans protect, nurture, and take care of themselves once born into the world — is perhaps the most prevalent womb symbol that exists. It is right up there in importance with caves, oceans, swallowing beasts — especially beasts of the ocean like whales (Jonah), sharks (*Jaws*), and octopi or giant squids.

There was a recent movie of this squid variation. Its plot development was of the *Jaws* genre. But in adding tentacles, it added elements of pubic hair and umbilical strangulation to the normal aspects of womb torture such as simple compression and suffocation.

House; cave; water; devouring dragon, as in Harry Potter; whale or shark; automobile, especially buses or motorhomes; boat, especially a submarine; indeed all vehicles of transition, nonmechanical as well as mechanical as in trains and airplanes; the deep forest, as in *Avatar* — anything in fact with elements of being surrounding and engulfing of one and as nurturing or threatening one, or both, are womb symbols, as we have known for a long time.

Prison, Jail Cell, Schoolroom = Womb

In the category of womb symbols that are places that enclose or "house" one that are uncomfortable, constricting, limiting of one's ability to move around and in which one is made to suffer, even be tortured, we need to add prisons, dungeons, jail cells, and schoolrooms. Breaking out of prisons, being rescued from tight, enclosing places or situations in which one is not free — that is, cannot "move freely" — are specific portrayals of the birth process itself. Contemporary film is flooded with plots and scenes depicting such escapes and/or rescues. Any constricting surround is a womb symbol, including oppressive social and political conditions from which one cannot escape and under which one is not able to move freely, to enjoy "freedom"; especially regimented ones under which one is tortured, processed, and treated anonymously and in an unfeeling, insensitive manner.

Schools and schoolrooms are especially strong womb symbols for they are places in which a person is supposedly nurtured and helped along in one's development, exactly as was the purpose and situation in the womb. Libraries are the benign version of womb-like "schooling" in that the element of volition or choice in the matter exists. When they depict being constricted or made to suffer, it becomes even more obvious, depicting as that does the later stages in the womb which are uncomfortable and often hellacious.

The Wall

In the school sequences in the movie, *The Wall*, there are other perinatal elements potentiating some of the scenes. We have anonymity, indicating not being seen in the womb; fetal faces; tortuous "development" and passage from one state to another especially as in being shoved through a wringer or meat grinder; and faces coming out of walls or having an appearance similar to that.

Houses and Spaceships Are Real "Mothers"

One lengthy explanation of this kind of symbolism as it is connected with "the Mother" is the classic work by the Jungian, Erich Neumann, titled, *The Origins and History of Consciousness*, which he himself based on other even earlier analyses of mother symbolism and its association with enclosing and enveloping sorts of thing.

At any rate, among all these, the house is probably the most popular symbol today. It would seem to be used more in the visual media as a womb symbol than any other, currently. With the increased interest in science fiction, the spaceship is perhaps coming in second, but even that distantly.

Being spaceships, UFOs are obviously womb symbols. Carl Jung once speculated in writing that the upsurge of UFO sightings indicated a rising urge for psychic unity in humans. While this is true on one level, on a deeper level, they are symbols of reintegration with our repressed traumatic womb experiences. Space travel is transition from one world to another in general. And the vehicle of passage is a UFO or spaceship … in which one's needs are taken care of and one is involved in passage or transition. It is not surprising that often in the course of this transition, space travel, the space voyagers of the silver screen encounter odd and horrifying developments.

Notice how we say "mother ship." UFO type spaceships are so often depicted as round or spherical. Indeed, we have elaborate developments of these themes in the Death Star depiction of *Star Wars* — a round enclosed place and habitat associated with dread and death.

"You Will Be Assimilated."

The variations on this are themselves telling. We have one instance of a cubical habitat in space ... a square, not round, spaceship. What better way to show how terrifyingly different the inhabitants are from natural, biological beings. For womb equals round, flowing lines as in Nature, products of a physical or biological world, one of life and dealing with living and animate things. Whereas to indicate that these beings are mechanical, unnatural, robotic ... products of a mental world only, one of death and dealing with inanimate, non-living things ... machines ... straight lines are employed, implying the worlds of engineering, mathematics, geometry ... of the mind only, not of the physical or biological worlds or the worlds of feeling and experience. Implying a world of non-feeling and non-experience is horrifyingly akin to implying a death-like existence.

Star Trek aficionados will have picked up by now I am referring to the Borg and to their cubical spaceships/habitats. We have to make the connection that the appearance of symbols of machines, robots, androids, and such with womb symbols — increasingly prevalent in modern and postmodern times — is easily attributable to the fact of our ever increasing mechanization of birth ... in which, as I was pointing out in the previous section, humans are "thingified" and turned into "human robots." And, yes, these are horrifying and death-like experiences that we undergo at our beginnings and subject our incoming members to.

Worse Homes and Gardens. Is It Any Wonder It Is Haunted?

I remember watching an old movie from the Amityville series. As most people are aware, in any of these movies, it is the evil house that is the source of the horror. This goes back at least to Edgar Allen Poe's *The House of Usher*.

Yet this plot idea of an evil house, which must, in the end, come crashing down in flames — indicating the explosive and fiery birth, BPM III, which signals the release from the evil forces —

was boringly evident in films in the Twentieth Century.

Mad Doctor Frankenstein, the Obstetrician

Related to this, taking this theme back in time, is the ideas of dungeons or castles … with mad scientists, no less — obstetricians, perhaps?

At any rate, in this idea of a house that "gobbles" one up, we have the bringing together of two of the most predominant birth elements in film — an evil house and a devouring beast. That fact of a doubling of perinatal elements alone is indicative of a plot saturated with perinatal influence.

Origins of Parallel Universes

But this idea of something coming through the walls, membrane walls, is both fascinating and telling in the extreme. It speaks to other perinatal elements and feelings.

I might start by pointing out the element of there being another realm into which people go and from which people are rescued (with luck). There is a barrier between the two realms — a permeable, elastic barrier. Anytime you have this other realm you are talking about either birth or death or both. Oftentimes it is both, for it is felt that to go back to the time of being in the womb ("regression") is akin to death.

Of course we get this idea that birth is death, for one thing, because of the fact that at that time — in the late stages of pregnancy with fetal malnutrition, lack of sufficient oxygen, suffocation, and so on — there was a sense of impending death, and oftentimes actual vital life threat to the fetus. We see our beginnings as dire, for another thing, because the actual time of being born is analogous to a dying to one state in order to be born into another. Actual birth,

BPM III, has most often been related to feelings of death/rebirth.

So of course, for these reasons, anything having to do with going across or back into that other realm is going to be associated with death.

"There's No Place Like Home."

But death is not the only aspect of crossing some kind of barrier into another realm. Related to the house theme we see how going through a membrane into another realm can take one into another place where one has adventures and rediscovers important understandings or is transformed or matured in some way.

In this category we have Alice going through a looking glass to go into Wonderland; Dorothy and Toto in *The Wizard of Oz* being transported — in their *house,* naturally — to another realm; and the back of the wardrobe opening up into the other land of Narnia in the classic children's series by C. S. Lewis titled, *The Lion, The Witch, and the Wardrobe.* In *Howl's Moving Castle,* a floating, traveling house takes the occupants to different places and into various adventures and scenes, like some kind of animated version of *Sliders.*

Through the Looking Glass

And of course this is only the tip of the iceberg of works of literature, film, and TV that could be given: the magic mirror, often an antique one (of course), which opens up to another horrible or wonderful place or to a time in the past; or the secret passageway in a wall that opens, by means of some magical or technical maneuver, and takes one into secret places — both wondrous and hideous.

The hearth that spins around is particularly telling in that the hearth may be considered the "heart" or center of the maternal in the house, the prime source of heat and nourishment — as when in previous times it was the place in which the food was actually cooked. There are many other examples.

The movie *Jumanji* with Robin Williams employed this idea laboriously and dramatically, with people going through walls into other times and places.

But the movie also included perinatal elements such as stampedes of gigantic jungle animals and even floods. Here again we see beasts that can devour or crush one, but also enveloping waters. In fact, when the flooding waters came through the wall, to accompany this element there was even the "mandatory" fight with a toothy beast!

This "Dark" Unknown

In this movie, *Jumanji*, as in too many others, the "other side" is depicted as a dangerous and often deathly place. This points to the vital life threat that we go through at the times of our birth, leaving an imprint of fear of it for a lifetime.

This depiction of it and fear of it are both understandable and unfortunate. For, as I alluded to earlier, this idea of birth trauma has been vigorously resisted in our culture ever since it was first presented by Otto Rank. And we can attribute that resistance to accepting its reality to the fact that it triggers so much fear in people to even consider these perinatal influences.

Love, Fear Relationship

To put it another way, considering, as we now are, how imbued with death, fear, and pain is this time of our life, we are capable of seeing that *there are good reasons why otherwise logical people would at all costs resist the idea of birth trauma and perinatal influences, the evidence be damned.* We are fascinated by this time of our life. We play it out endlessly in our imaginations and collective dreams and, as we shall see in the next chapter, in our everyday lives. But we are utterly terrified of it. Indeed it is, as Janov once put it, the only time for most people that in life we come so close to death, other than our actual demise.

To Hell With It …

So to acknowledge birth is to face death and an inner memory of horror and a hell-like experience. These aspects of it are not going to lend to its being readily accepted among our intellectual currency.

Clients in the therapy rooms only face their perinatal memories when all other interpretations, memories, and early experiences have been made and integrated. The perinatal is the last and most gruesome of truths to face. It is faced only when all other options are gone and the truth alone will do.

In the same way — since it is not easy truth — its acceptance into the arena of our common knowledge has awaited its *necessity* to be known and acknowledged. It has required our species survival being at stake for us to consider the deepest roots of our problems.[3]

Face Me, or You're Mine!

And this book is primarily about that necessity to face the ultimate and horrible truths if we are to save ourselves. Not only are we closer to our perinatal unconscious these days, we are — because of the precarious nature of our times, which our ignorance and denial of the perinatal heretofore has set up for us — required to face the perinatal "monster" or we are doomed. It is now the time to uncover the truth, to get to the root of the problem, or there will simply, eventually, *be* no problem, because there will be no people to have a problem or to recognize a truth or root of a problem.

Fear and Freedom … Only a Membrane Away

Be that as it may, this recent development in perinatal imagery involving a membrane barrier between us and the perinatal realm is closer to our actual perinatal reality than any of the previous symbols put out in earlier times which showed a barrier between us and the perinatal. So this membrane depiction of the perinatal suggests an increasing closeness to the perinatal unconscious.

Perinatal Spamming

We have progressed in our collective consciousness beyond hard walls or mirrors separating us from our perinatal memories (and horror), now they are just a membrane away. They are only a thin, elastic membrane away. And from the other side this part of ourselves calls out to us, pushing its face through — like the computer *push* technology, with all its annoying pop-up consoles and screens that won't go away. Our births come spamming through to tell us what we need and to call us back to a realization of the truths we need to hear to save ourselves.

Getting back to the membrane symbol itself, the perinatal elements of this new depiction are rife. Obviously the late stages of pregnancy have one in an enclosed elastic, membrane container — the womb — from which one cannot escape. Also, the fetus's features in the latest stages are somewhat evident, can be seen and felt, on the surface of the mother's belly, something like faces pushing out of elastic walls. And one struggles agonizingly during birth and endures intense suffocation through a great deal of it, just like those in movies who are surrounded by elastic sheets.

All of this is then, in Western civilization, compounded after birth with tight swaddling. The newborn, curiously, is wrapped like a tamale in a way that he or she cannot move freely. So rather than remember the earlier womb experience of blissful freedom and euphoria, it has its most recent hellish experience of the late stages of gestation and birth reinforced. There is no doubt that we are letting our newest members know they will not be able to move freely in life, have freedom, or express themselves freely. It is no wonder that depression is pandemic in modern society and antidepressants are sprinkled over the masses like holy water.

Baby Abductees and Masked Medical Aliens

Finally, a later perinatal element is inserted in the *Fire In the Sky* scene in that the struggling abductee, covered in the elastic membrane sheet, is lying on an alien's medical table. In the same way a baby, right after birth, endures the struggle for breath, caused by premature umbilical cutting, as it lies on the medical table and receives "processing" by medical personnel who to the fetus are alien-looking — that is, they have prominent eyes and lower face not pronounced because covered with surgical mask.

The point of bringing out the occurrence of these media images is that the projective systems of our culture — our art — are reflecting our collective changes in consciousness: Specifically, the evolution of our consciousness as it is confronted by this unconscious pre- and perinatal material ... or, as some psychohistorians would have it, the "collapsing" of our "ego strength" as we are "threatened" by these "dangerous" perinatal elements.

Birthing Into Everyday Life

Whether these images are indicative of a healing crisis or are the opening of a Pandora's box — that is to say, Earth rebirth or apocalypse — will be something for us to consider further on.

Meanwhile, let us look at how these elements, not only show up in our collective media dreams, but fashion the very furniture of our everyday reality.

CHAPTER 4

TWENTY-FIRST CENTURY AND ITS DISCONTENTS

Dangling Above an Abyss

Beyond the entertainment media, it seems perinatal themes and elements are showing up everywhere else in our surrounding environment and culture. The scenery of our everyday reality consists of pollution of our air, water, and food; threat of death "at any moment," caused by the knowledge of the power of nuclear weapons; fantasies of apocalypse of all kinds, magnified, perhaps, by the ending of a millennium and the approach of the end of the Mayan calendar in 2012 — including fundamentalist Christian imaginings of an end to human civilization in an apocalyptic "rapture"; New Age fantasies of ecological, spiritual, and social utopias; and so on.

First, let us consider a few of the most blatantly birth-related of the events around us.

The Primal Screen: Aliens … Ooooooooooo … Sca-ry … .

Alien abduction stories, while a relatively recent addition to our cultural landscape, are unusual in the rapidity with which they have gained cultural currency and are telling in the extreme fascination the public has with them. They have catapulted more than one show — *The X Files* being the prime example, of course — to cult-like status

Fetal Aliens

Yet Alvin Lawson has pointed out how alien abduction stories are replete with perinatal elements: passing through walls, umbilical beams of connection to the "mother ship" — the placenta — either fetal-looking aliens or aliens whose eyes are most prominent and the lower parts of their faces undistinguished — similar to the way a newborn might see an obstetrician wearing a medical mask.

Then of course there are the elements of being medically probed, measured, samples taken from one, and being swooshed from one place to another with no say on one's part — all remarkably like the experience of a newborn, right out of the womb.[1]

Pretty Much

While I do not think that the "alien abduction" phenomenon is just derivative of birth, as Lawson does, I do believe that we perceive these events through a veil of birth trauma, the likes of which the world has never known. My position is explained in the online article, "Alien Abductors: Angelic Midwives or Hounds From Hell?"

Mouth Suctioning ... "Oh, What Pretty Teeth You Have, My Alien"

An interesting development in the alien face is the "shoved down the throat" thing going on. Similar to the *Jacob's Ladder* kind of vegetable thrusting out, which was described in the last chapter, it was popularized greatly in the movie, *Alien.*

As a neonate we cannot see the mouths of the masked attendants at our birth. In a traumatic situation, whatever is hidden is more feared than what can be seen. As in anything else, onto the unknown we can project the most magnified versions of our fears. When these images arise in us, then, it makes sense that if the mouth is shown it might be even more frightening than that above the mouth.

So in modern times, for the first time in history, we see something going on where these feelings are symbolized as a ferocious mouth coming out of the mouth. The fact that it appears like something that would gag reveals that this image contains elements of the trauma around ungentle mouth suctioning or clearing as well as the reveal of what might be under the mask of the seeming attacker, the obstetrician. Add lots of teeth and you have the perinatal *vagina dentate* as well, symbolizing the trauma occurring at birth, when actually emerging from the mother.

The Perinatal Veil: Rock Concerts (For some, ditto)

Lawson has also described perinatal elements in rock concerts.[2]

Mosh Wombs

Keep in mind that rock music popularity and concert rituals are world-wide phenomena. Youth from nearly all countries are involved in rock culture. Among other things, Lawson, in his article, refers to placental guitars, umbilical mikes, and youths jumping into mosh pits. Mosh pits suggest birth feelings in that they simulate the crushing in the womb.

At birth our consciousness is filled with the feeling of flesh all around. The world is crushing, heaving, rollicking, bouncing flesh everywhere. During a non-cesarean birth one struggles and moves through this flesh to reach space, air, light ... freedom. We re-create this pattern of struggle in order to reach the light, or freedom and space, throughout life. It is obvious that mosh pits are attractive, appealing places to re-create the danger of birth alongside the hope of being "held up," uplifted, and reborn.

The Doors of Perception ... Stormed

We could also mention the loud music, fireworks, and flashing and bright explosions of light at these concerts as perinatal in that they re-create the assault of sensation that occurs to the newly emerged fetus — an assault which in one's mind is like unto a bomb exploding.

The rock groups and their lyrics themselves are often blatantly perinatal. The most obvious example of this was the group, Nirvana, who came out with a CD titled "In Utero." The fact that the leader of the group, Kurt Cobain, committed suicide is a strong indication of his closeness and access to his perinatal trauma ... as I will soon explain.

Pacifiers, Trolls, and Collective Rebirth

Turning from rock, we see perinatal BPM III elements in the scenery of our everyday lives evident in the rising incidence of violence by children at ever younger ages.

In Europe, as pointed out by Mayr and Boederl, it appears a

collective regression to the perinatal is going on, especially among the youth.[3]

Collective Navel-Gazing

The forms this "regression" has taken include the surprising popularity of a pop song, sung by a very young child, expressing the difficulties of being a baby; the wearing of baby pacifiers as ornaments as a powerful fashion fad; and being enamored of troll-like dolls, which, according to the authors indicate a "regression to the womb."

I would say a *progression* to the womb, by the way.... I will soon explain why.

Overpopulation Bring Up in Us Uncomfortable Claustrophobic Feelings From Our Births

We have no-exit, claustrophobic BPM II elements manifesting in the crushing populations in major cities throughout the world.

In the later stages of our womb lives, we are increasingly compressed with flesh all around. It is a time of ever more compression, constriction, restriction of movement, suppression of freedom, and suffering, which seems unending. However uncomfortable, we are compelled to manifest similar situations in our later adult lives, as in creating our crowded cities. We then find ourselves triggered into feelings like the ones we had back then.

Though it is irrational to draw suffering to oneself, it makes psychic sense in that consciousness seeks to integrate that which was overwhelming at the time. Think of this as a memory of a dire threat to one's life that a part of ourselves remembers and tries to remove as a threat to our well-being by drawing it to ourselves repeatedly in life until we have managed to accept it — deal with it, perceive it differently than being a threat — so that we can go beyond it.

For the psyche's main goal is to grow and heal itself. We see this intention of consciousness manifest in observing the body that Consciousness creates and which we see, which does exactly that growing and healing throughout life. Consciousness seeks, always, greater consciousness. Consciousness seeks unity.

Earlier we looked into how we do that seeking of psychological healing at rock concerts and with their mosh pits, in particular.

So we unconsciously create situations in life that make us feel like we once did but could not deal with at the time. And these feelings of course are uncomfortable ... why else could we not deal with them originally? This does not mean that by bringing suffering to us we solve it and accept it. We would not be bringing it repeatedly to us if we successfully got beyond it.

No, we create suffering such as overpopulation because we are NOT dealing with, accepting, resolving, facing the memories that are making us continually manifest situations that should remind us ... but don't. What to do about this — and how this might be hopeful for solving the biggest problems of all on Earth — is what I deal with in time in this work. But I digress. Stay tuned, though.

The Perinatal Pulls of Pollution: Air Pollution and Fetal Oxygen Starvation

Increased Carbon Dioxide, But Also Decreased Oxygen

One overlooked, but hugely pervasive perinatal element of these strange days is connected to the increasing carbon dioxide concentration in our atmosphere called "the greenhouse effect" which occurs alongside the curiously overlooked yet necessarily corresponding decreases in oxygen levels. There is increasingly less oxygen as we use it up burning carbon-based fossil fuels and making carbon dioxide.[4]

We have more carbon dioxide for that reason and also because we are stupidly destroying the Earth's mechanisms for turning that carbon dioxide back into oxygen … forests and ocean plankton, for example. This increased carbon dioxide is called "the greenhouse effect." While this has been looked at from the perspective of it creating global warming and climate change, there are even stronger corporate (profit-motivated) as well as personal psychological reasons why we do not look at its most immediate effect on humans — the amount of oxygen we get from the air we breathe. We will steal at least a brief glance into some psychological reasons now and while we are at it uncover rich veins of understanding of and possible solutions for not only our current environmental problems but certain political and social dilemmas which we will find are operating dialectically with them. For there are provocative and profound influences from our experiences in the late stages of our womb life on the kaleidoscope of our current postmodern lives.

Air Pollution Bring Up in Us Uncomfortable Feelings from Our Births

For the increased carbon dioxide and reduced oxygen of the globe is analogous to the situation of "fetal malnutrition," described by Briend and deMause, that occurs prior to birth, and which is the basis for deMause's explanation of poisonous placenta symbolism. Keep in mind in particular that we experience this reduction in oxygen and increase in carbon dioxide in the form of air pollution, which is most pronounced in larger cities.[5]

Perinatal Arising in Sixties and Generations Since

Other evidence for closeness to the perinatal unconscious comes from Kenneth Keniston, who studied the youth of the Sixties. In Keniston's widely read book of the time titled *The Uncommitted: Alienated Youth in American Society*, he described an increasingly prevalent, unusually influential, and relatively newly emerging personality type, which he discovered in his sociopsychological study of youthful college students.

Raging to Reenter, Digging Under Ground, Fantasy of Fusion

Among other traits, he found these youth to be characterized by fantasies of a "rage to reenter" the womb; and a "fantasy of fusion" with the mother, which took perinatal forms of all kinds including stories of wishing to dig one's way back into the earth; a fascination with and wish to return to the past, the long forgotten, and the under ground; and a desire to find oblivion in some enveloping medium ... even at the price of self-destruction!

Existential Angst, Death and Dying, Peter Pan

Some of the other noticeably perinatal elements of Sixties youth were existential angst, being enamored of death and dying, and a refusal of "normal" adulthood. (See BPM I, BPM II, and BPM II.) And think about it. Are these descriptions also not a lot like what we have heard of the generation that followed Sixties youth ... the so-called Generation X?

Vampire Apocalypse ... It's All So Black and White

For Generation X, black clothes, white painted faces, and black lipstick were the fashion statement of the Eighties and Nineties.

And what was this statement of that sector of Gen X youth — a statement that began in the Seventies among what was then called the "punk" movement, which includes now the fad of vampirism — except the same fascination with death as Sixties "alienated" youth ... again. This mental set is an obvious reflection of the death/rebirth aspects of the perinatal I have been discussing. The "perinatal veil" through which they saw things was becoming more blatant.

Being Gratefully Dead

But this trend began with the Boomer Generation. Need I remind of this same theme of being dead and then reborn coming from the Sixties as in being "gratefully dead"? It seems that this trend toward easier access to and higher awareness of perinatal influences has been going on for a while now.

A Perinatal Printout Is Indicated by Drug Use

There are other perinatal similarities between the youth of the Sixties and the generations to follow — this time specifically with the Millennial Generation, the one that followed Gen X and who are predominantly the sons and daughters of Boomer parents. Millennials were born after the mid-Seventies; they are a different cohort from those born 1960 till roughly 1974 — Gen X; and those born 1945 to 1959 — the Boomers.

Drug Usage Rising Since the Nineties Shows Perinatal Attraction

Illegal drug use among youth, beginning in the Nineties, began going up again. This coincides with the coming into young adulthood of the Millennial Generation. Unlike drug usage of the legal and mind-debilitating kind (booze and tobacco), drug usage of the illegal and mind-facilitating kind (pot, LSD, speed, ecstasy) is an indication of an emerging perinatal unconscious. Drugs are intimately woven with perinatal influences in a number of ways. Not only can some drugs bring up birth feelings, as Grof's work has shown, but the mother being drugged while giving birth to her child can result in drug abuse by that child later in life.

Millennials Are Sixty-ish

There is another overlooked factor or aspect of this rise in drug use in the Nineties by Millennials: These youngsters were the sons and daughters of the Sixties generation who, in their own youth, as we all know too well, engaged in drug experimentation. In fact, this younger generation of drug users has sometimes been called the baby-boomer "echo" generation.

Gen Xers Are Fifty-ish

Millennials are quite a bit different from the previous "echo" generation — Gen X. The generation that came to age during the Eighties — Yuppies and Xers — had parents who were born during the Great Depression and World War Two, who had their young adult formative years during the Eisenhower-McCarthy-Presley Fifties. So Gen X was influenced by their parents to conservatism, career-mindedness, and, for drug-of-choice, alcohol.

But this "echo" generation of Millennials has parents whose young adulthood was forged in the rebellion, drug and sex experimentation, activism, liberal-radicalism, and idealism of the Sixties, not the Fifties.[6]

Forget What You've Heard About Generation Gap

Generationally speaking, we know that children do not

predominantly rebel to the opposite of their parents' values. Kenneth Keniston, for one, has made it clear — referring to studies — that children are paramountly influenced by the values and attitudes ... conscious and unconscious ... of their parents. So this most recent cohort of youth was of course going to be more liberal in their attitude to drug use than Gen X, even if their parents, in their coming into adulthood, overtly decry or are against the use of drugs. Keep in mind also that many of the baby-boomers have retained, not reversed, their acceptance of drug experimentation, and many still believe in and use drugs; many still considering the occasional use of certain types — especially the psychedelics, and to some extent, pot — to be an aid to self-development and/or spiritual awareness.

Family Lies Not "Family Ties"

The myth that youth rebel against their parents' values was expressed and propagandized by the TV show "Family Ties." This was an oh-so-convenient portrayal, as it contributed to the pervasive scapegoating of the Sixties generation by the Fifties Generation — the Eisenhower-McCarthy-Presley generation — who came into their Triumphant Phase, that is, took over the reins of society as mature adults in the Eighties.

Rebellion in Youth Amounts to Being Uncompromising About Parents' Values Not Defying Them

This "Family Ties" kind of rebellion, however inaccurate, seems to be credible largely as a result of the observation that youth do rebel against their parents. But it ignores the fact that when they do, and they don't always, they revolt or rebel, as in the Sixties youth, most often in the direction of being more insistent of actually living the values of their parents, not simply voicing them. As Keniston found out, for example, as he described in his follow-up to *The Uncommitted*, in the book, *Young Radicals: Notes on Committed Youth*, radical youth had liberal (hardly conservative!) parents.

When Sixties youth were angry at their parents it was out of their perception of their parents as compromising and not living out their own expressed ideals, as laid out to their children in raising them. Therefore, Sixties rage against adults came out of their disgust at their parents for "not walking their talk." As we may recollect, there was the oft-repeated charge of "hypocrite" directed by some of these youth toward their parental generation.

Millennials and Their Sixties Parents

In this regard notice also that this latest crop of young — born mid-70s through roughly 2000 (Boomers had children over a longer expanse of time than generations previous and since, for reasons that I've dealt with in other places) and being now in their twenties and thirties ... the sons and daughters of the Sixties Generation — has also seen increases in voting for liberal or Democratic candidates. Their turnout for Clinton in 1992 was the first time since the Seventies that the youth vote went Democratic. Their support of Obama was widely given as the reason for his success.

Occupy Wall Street ... Sixties Gen Liberals, Millennial Revolutionaries?

In the Nineties we saw — despite the AIDS scare — an end to a fledgling "youth celibacy movement" — which had been a movement of Yuppie/Gen Xers encouraged by their Fifties Generation parents. The Millennials, echoing again their parents and this time the sexual revolution, were noted for early and/or increased sexual experimentation. This latest cohort of youth also has seen increases in idealism, activism, and volunteerism. It is no coincidence that we have finally seen a rising up of activism again in the Occupy Wall Street movement, with Millennials taking the lead and supported, taught, and inspired by their Sixties cohort parents.[7]

The Epidemic of Depression Shows Pervasive BPM II Influence

Lucy in the Sewer with Depression

Other connections between drug use and perinatal influence: Perinatal feelings are very often of the depressive, no-exit type, and some drugs are temporarily effective antidotes for that. Depression itself is epidemic nowadays, indicating the rise of BPM II feelings. There is widespread use of antidepressants in America currently.

No-Exit Wombs

Stanislav Grof has claimed, based upon the tens of thousands of sessions of exploration into the perinatal unconscious that he has personally facilitated and thus observed, that the roots of endogenous — that is to say, deep rooted and engrained, not just situational — depression lie in the no-exit BPM II experience in the womb prior to birth. Furthermore, my personal experience with depression earlier in my life and my primal re-experiencing of prenatal, womb feelings, as well as birth, confirms his statement.

Psychedelics and Birth: Tune Inward, Turn Back, Drop Down

Finally, psychedelic drugs ... LSD ... "they're ba-a-a-ack." Though they are more discreetly used these days and so are less obviously evident. Various psychedelics and hallucinogens are used at postmodern raves, among many other places.

Their increased use also points to perinatal influences in that it is known that psychedelics — LSD in particular — can help people to access and to some extent resolve perinatal trauma, when taken for purposes of personal growth.

Corrective on LSD Misinformation

For those who have cynically adopted the line that either psychedelics are another drug that blots out one's Pain or that they are only used for recreational or sensual/hedonistic purposes or that the kinds of birth experiences that Grof describes as occurring on LSD only occur in supervised and guided sessions, like the ones he offered ... for those who have dismissed psychedelics and LSD in any of these ways, let me say the following:

LSD is Hardly Escapist

First, psychedelics, especially LSD and to some extent, even marijuana, are known to act in the brain in a way almost exactly the opposite of the drugs used to escape from reality — such as, for example, alcohol, nicotine, or heroin — though this news flies in the face of the myth put out by the all-encompassing anti-drug propaganda machine, which puts all drugs in the same category. This is common knowledge among researchers and scientists who study these things. For elaboration, see "Culture War, Class War Chapter Three: Drugs and Generations — Opposing Worlds" — especially the part on "Drugs and Consciousness" — as well as subsequent chapters of that book/blog.[8]

Drugs — Not Just for Fun Anymore

Second, that drugs are only used for recreational purposes is patently false. Though the vast majority of drug use is recreational, there are in print many examples, and the admissions of many authors, of the use of LSD by individuals and groups for purposes of personal growth. And, in my own limited exploration, personal growth was my motivation. In fact, many people are afraid to take the drug LSD, knowing full well that its effects are not always pleasurable or recreational. So why would they accept that risk if they did not have some other intent, like personal growth, for experimenting on themselves with it?

LSD and Birth Reliving

Finally, before I had ever heard of such a possibility of reliving one's birth, let alone heard of Grof, or Janov for that matter, I learned that at least one person at my university on LSD found himself feeling like a fetus and then going through a process of struggling through a birth canal, and so on.

"Most Peculiar, Mama!"

In this book so far, we have considered the uniqueness of our times and the elements of the perinatal unconscious. We have followed that with a look at the predominant underlying fantasies and myths of our times — our contemporary collective dreams as projected onto the silver screen, boob tube, and printed page, with a perinatal rock heartbeat of a soundtrack.

Our Nightly News and Neighborhoods

Finally we have taken a look at the anomalous elements of our everyday reality — those confusing and bizarre, newly emerging images that permeate our nightly news and neighborhoods, along with those totally unprecedented cultural, environmental, and social factors that weave the backdrops of our lives.

Going Forward, Explore Our Hells and Heavens

Let us now go deeper. Let us make the connections. Let us explore the way we have reflected our innermost intimate hells and heavens into the fabric of our times. And back again, let us uncover the way the warp and woof of these strangest of days has affected each of us, in our most superficial of behaviors to the most intimate and deepest of our minds. The way forward is down.

CHAPTER 5

BIRTH WARS, WORLD WOES

We Interrupt This Book for a Breaking News Bulletin: "Hellacious Birth Traumas Making Headlines Worldwide!" Film at Eleven.

The connections between the physical conditions and symbols discussed in previous chapters and the perinatal unconscious should be obvious and may have already to some extent been spelled out. But let me finish connecting the dots, so to speak:

As Stanislav Grof put it,

We have exteriorized in the modern world many of the essential themes of the perinatal processes that a person involved in deep personal transformation has to face and come to terms with internally. The same elements that we would encounter in the process of psychological death and rebirth in our visionary experiences make today our evening news.

This is particularly true in regard to the phenomena that characterize what I call BPM III.

We certainly see the enormous unleashing of the aggressive impulse in the many wars and revolutionary upheavals in the world, in the rising criminality, terrorism, and racial riots. Sexual experiences and behaviors are taking unprecedented forms, as manifested in sexual freedom of youngsters, promiscuity, open marriages, overtly sexual books, plays, and movies, gay liberation, sadomasochistic experimentation, and many others. The demonic element is also becoming increasingly manifest in the modern world.

A renaissance of satanic cults and witchcraft, the popularity of books and horror movies with occult themes, and crimes with satanic motivations attest to that fact. The scatological dimension is evident in the progressive industrial pollution, accumulation of waste products on a global scale, and rapidly deteriorating hygienic conditions in large cities[1]

Grof is saying, then, that we have manifested an external modern world that mirrors and re-creates some of the hellacious circumstances surrounding our traumatic human births.

No-Exit Car Jams and People Clusters

In addition to the myriad of ways that Grof has detailed ... and there are many more he could have mentioned ... I would like to add a few obvious commonplace examples.

We re-create on a daily basis in major cities the no-exit frustration-depression-rage prior to birth in the traffic jams and gridlock of commuter traffic.

Another one: the population explosion. Simple overpopulation of the globe sets up scenarios exactly analogous to the negative conditions that existed toward the end of pregnancy when we grew/expanded too much to be any longer comfortable in the womb. The way this global overpopulation impacts us: the overpopulation and frenzy in a big city, manifesting the situation of a crushing womb.

Global "Therapeutic" Carbon-Dioxide Chamber

I have already mentioned reduced oxygen in the atmosphere and its relation to fetal "malnutrition."

However, there is an interesting sidelight to this. For both Arthur Janov and Stanislav Grof, at one time early on, experimented with a technique of carbon dioxide ingestion for getting people into primal and perinatal states. In fact, at the time — in the late Sixties, early Seventies — though not on a large scale, a number of professionals were experimenting with this procedure and even offering it as a means of "expanding consciousness."

The point is that increased carbon dioxide and decreased oxygen naturally stimulate perinatal feelings. Lucky us, as we continue to turn the entire atmosphere of the Earth into such a "therapeutic" carbon-dioxide chamber.

"Don't Cut Me OFF, Man!"

After all this, if you still do not believe that a perinatal unconscious is emerging at this time in history, I ask you how else to explain how the simple act of being "cut off" in traffic can trigger so much perinatal "no exit" frustration as to enrage an "otherwise normal" person to pull out a gun and blow another's life away. Incidentally, I myself had a shotgun pulled on me in such a situation and only escaped through a high-speed car chase.

Birth Wars ~ World Woes

The upshot of it all is that somehow or other we have managed to create a world situation that mirrors in a way unlike any other time in history our perinatal imprints and thus triggers the emergence of this perinatal unconscious.

Or, you might reverse that and say that an emerging perinatal unconscious — brought about by other factors, improved "child-caring" methods perhaps ... more about that later — has resulted in our creating a world situation manifesting or acting out those unconscious perinatal elements, which are having increasing influence on our consciousness and on our behavior.

I suspect both of these processes are occurring — each one augmenting the other.

Noticing Our Underbellies

Let me make this latter scenario clearer. What I am saying is that we all have birth trauma and we must distance ourselves from this birth trauma so that we can function. If the birth trauma is extreme, or if subsequent child-caring is abusive and neglectful[2] — as is the case in any of the "less enlightened" of deMause's psychogenic modes of child-rearing[3] — or both, then complete splitting, repression of the perinatal, and dissociation from the perinatal occurs. Thus a person can project his or her perinatal unconscious onto the world and be completely unaware that it has anything to do with him- or herself.

Can You Look Your Belly in the Face?

However, with more humane child-caring modes — deMause's latest psychogenic mode, for example[3] — less repression, and less defenses, are necessary and total dissociation does not occur. In this situation, the perinatal is not completely projected onto the outside world. We have more access to it, hence we act it out and manifest it in lesser ways, which reflect back to us, for the times when we are able to see them, our perinatal underbellies.

On the one hand, the world is becoming increasingly perinatal and thus is stimulating more of the perinatal unconscious than previously. On the other hand, we have more access to and are closer to our perinatal unconscious so that we exhibit it more blatantly in our behavior and cultural creations and thus stimulate, again, in ourselves and others, the underlying perinatal matrices.

This is a chicken-and-the-egg process. And I suspect, in the same way, that these processes are going on simultaneously and hence augment each other.

Life or Death Matters

In Chapter One, "Strange Days," we entertained the notion that the reason things seem so much different nowadays than anytime we can imagine from the past is because they *are* different. We have looked at how the character and events of our age are remarkably like the feelings and events surrounding our births and, unfortunately: traumatic births, traumatic times! Lastly, we have considered a few reasons ... more coming ... as to why these times might be uniquely imbued with our perinatal events.

"Waiter, Check!"

Still, the biggest questions lie begging: What does this all mean for us? Is it the "end of the world," really, like some are claiming? Or are we seeing the "dawning of a new age"? (Now why is it that I cannot restrain the strains of the group The Fifth Dimension, in full orchestration no less, intoning in my mind the song "The Age of Aquarius" as I write this!?)

What Can You Me Do?

These are not unimportant questions. And they have all the implications of life or death, again indicative of the perinatal, about them.

Will we live? Will we survive? Or are we doomed? Kinda important to think about, don't you agree?

And if it is within our power to decide our fate, well, just what the hell are we going to do about it? What can be done about our situation? What can each of us — you ... me — do?

What It Is That's Happening Here

We will begin addressing these questions in "Part Two: What It Is That Is Happening Here," beginning with the next chapter. There are some processes of change in these times — processes of change unlike any that we normally encounter — that will weigh heavily on the outcome of the current emerging perinatal unconscious. These include not only the concepts and processes of the healing crisis — or as stipulated in the next chapter, "Healing Crisis — Getting 'Sick' to Be Well" — but also that of macrocosmic processes beyond our human scope, as will be explained in "Chapter Seven: Through Gaia's Eyes — Nature Balances HerSelf."

Apocalypse, Or Earth Rebirth?

Finally, having considered the perinatal nature of our times in "Part One, The Perinatal Unconscious" (Chapters One through Five), and then the corresponding unique processes at work in these times in "Part Two, What It Is That Is Happening Here" (Chapters Six and Seven), we can look at some likely propensities for our future. Considering what we know at that time, we will see that there are also some directions in which to look for a solution. We will then be able to look deeper, daring to ask: Apocalypse? Or Earth Rebirth?

But next we need to consider how in order to save ourselves we need to bring to the surface all the rotten ugliness of perinatal trauma that for millennia our species has been keeping inside.

PART TWO

WHAT IT IS THAT IS HAPPENING HERE

CHAPTER 6

HEALING CRISIS — GETTING "SICK" TO BE WELL

Getting Sick In Order to Get Well

What does this all mean? What does this portend? What might be the outcome of this emerging perinatal unconscious? In other words, consciousness evolution or apocalypse?

To answer what an emerging perinatal unconscious might mean on a macrocosmic or societal-global scale, it is helpful to look at what an emerging perinatal unconscious portends on the individual or microcosmic level.

What we have learned from the experiential modalities — holotropic breathwork™, primal therapy, rebirthing, vivation, and others like them — is that unerringly people need to get "sicker" before they can get well. This should not be news to psychoanalysts or any of the other mainstream psychotherapists or counselors either.

69

Healing Crisis

Basically, the underlying repressed material must come to the "surface," must become more conscious … and obviously when it becomes more conscious its accompanying symptoms are exacerbated. This can be called a *healing crisis* in that the symptoms get worse, more obvious, more blatant; and there is a period of acting them out before integration and resolution happens.

One Must "Die" to One's Sickness Before One Can Be "Born" Well

When Grof talks about birth/death scenarios in the perinatal unconscious, he is including these sorts of healings, where one must "die" to one's sickness before one can be "reborn" into another way of being, without those sick patterns or symptoms.

Degrees of Disease

Dissociation — Completely Split Off

It's YOU! YOU're the f&^$#r!

We see a progression over the last century in which there was complete dissociation from the perinatal unconscious by those of the Fifties, the World-War-Two, and previous generations — hence complete projection of it on The Other — to lesser dissociations from it by the generations since, baby-boomer and afterward, which involve more awareness of it as being a part of oneself and less projection of it on The Other.

Wounded Deer

In this latter instance, there is more suffering from it and more individual acting out of it, so that in a sense one appears "sicker" — the perinatal is more obvious in one's behavior, taking more individual forms, and it is more easily recognized and seen to be a personal problem ... a "sickness." Earlier I described this consciousness as being the way of the centaur, for it reflects Chiron, in ancient myths, having an ongoing wound but eventually becoming a teacher and healer.

To understand the ways the perinatal manifests depending upon one's "closeness" to it, let us contrast the two extremes of being split off from it and being close to it.

Being Really Sick, But Denying It: WWII Generation, Nazis, KKK, Right Wing, Tea Party

Can't Know That You Don't Know

First let us take a look at what the perinatal appears like when it is completely split off from one's conscious personality. This complete splitting off from the perinatal entails a complete repression and denial of it. Consequently, one has absolutely no access to it, and thus one is in total ignorance of the underlying motivations of one's actions. One unconsciously acts out perinatal elements and traumas and manifests them in one's behavior, rationalizing all the while that one has really good — non-perinatal, "real world" — reasons for why one is doing the things one is doing.

What"s in Your Head, Zombie?

Psychohistorians deem this state to be such an oblivious one that they use the term *trance-state* for it, fully intending all the implications and connotations that term engenders. That is, they are saying that people who are this repressed and split off do their acting zombie-like and out of motivations completely hidden to themselves.[1]

Birth Woes ~ World Wars

In such total ignorance, and of course being totally ignorant that one is in ignorance, people in the past century have been able to act out their perinatal underbellies in ways to make such hideous and all-encompassing wars as World War I and World War II possible.

Leaving aside for a moment the myriad ways the perinatal has unconsciously been acted out in this century in creating the current situation in which we are on the brink of extinction — which can be considered the most serious consequences of this splitting off imaginable — simply focusing on this century's major wars as evidence of perinatal acting-out alone is instructive.

The Nazis, in particular, were extreme in their dissociation from their perinatal, in their projection of it onto the Jews, and their consequent ability to act it out in horrific ways on them and others. Alice Miller and Lloyd deMause have each detailed the psychodynamics of this projection of primal pain — both perinatal and childhood — in the creation of the people that Adolf Hitler and the Nazis became in their adulthood.[2]

The Nazis present us with the patterns of these processes of dissociation and projection in blatant and obvious relief. The way Nazis, especially in concentration camps, acted out perinatal trauma on their prisoners has been described in great detail by Grof as well.[3]

Being "Weller," But Appearing Sicker — Generations Since

As I said, contrasted with being completely split off — dissociated

— from one's perinatal unconscious, as the Fifties and WWII Generation are predominantly, is being less cut off from it and having some access to its energies. This means that rather than being totally and blindly driven by these forces, which are acting on one *indirectly*, one actually feels them somewhat: One has a sense of their being a *part* of one's experience as opposed to living within them so thoroughly that one has not a clue of their existence.

This means that one has more options than to act them out, but it also means they make one aware of one's perinatal sickness. One feels them, suffers from them, struggles with them.

On the other hand, one does not suffer or struggle from unconscious energies that one is compliant with and that are completely manifest and supported in one's social and cultural environments (for example, the worlds of the WWII and previous generations), however destructive that makes one's actions.

Trancing Versus Suffering

This difference may be likened to the difference between being a fish in water and totally oblivious to that fact versus living out of water and experiencing a downpour. When one is in less of a trance state, one is aware of alternative ways of being; in the example, that would be being dry. Consequently, one suffers and struggles amidst these forces and options ... and one has at least some ability to choose one's actions.

I do not believe it is simply coincidence that we are currently going from the Piscean Age — symbolized by fish in water — to the Aquarian Age — symbolized by a water bearer. This change was a big part of the consciousness during the Sixties, and I think we are beginning to see why: Going from a state where one is oblivious to the forces around one to a state where one can see the things one is dealing with (carrying the water) is no small thing.

It seems everything about evolution in humans has something to do with being between two mediums and the advance/the added perspective that comes with that, going all the way back to being the only ape to take to the water so much as to become partly aquatic — placing our species between water and land, halfway between a dolphin and a chimpanzee. I think we are heading toward being like the fairies and angels we imagine — halfway between land and air — but that is a whole other publication of mine.

Another analogy I have heard of this difference between the two modes of being completely oblivious and somewhat aware of one's unconscious is that between living full-time in an arctic environment where one has to wear a heavy coat versus living in a milder climate. In the warmer climes, one is both aware of what it is like to not have a coat — one has capacity to feel better ways of being — as well as how bulky, obstructing, and uncomfortable it is to have the coat on — suffering more from it, suffering from one's perinatal memories. Finally one is better able to decide when to have it on and not — one has more options. At some point I will discuss what this has to do with the increase of bipolar disorders, but not now.

One analogy I find especially provocative is the difference between watching a movie and being fully engrossed in it so that one does not know it is a movie, which is equivalent to acting out unconsciously from one's early imprints. Compare this to watching the same movie with equal interest, but being aware that one is in a theater. You can see where in the second instance one would feel there are more options; and one would feel that one could step back before finding oneself caught up in horrific actions.

Wounded Deer and Centaurs

However, being aware of one's discomfort (having "more access" to the perinatal), one suffers like the wounded deer — the innocent who feels things and so struggles with society's sickness that many others are unconsciously perpetrating. But, with time and success in handling this pain, one can become the wounded *healer* — the Centaur.

Now, why and how would this occur? As I have said, some access to the perinatal and more blatant and direct acting it out is exhibited by many of the baby-boomer generation. This is in large part due to their having been raised in a way that required less in the way of ego defenses to keep their primal pain suppressed. Psychohistorians like Glen Davis and Lloyd deMause have detailed a slow advance of child-caring techniques, with generations since the WWII Generation being raised with more attention to their needs and less harshness and cruelty ... increasingly more love.

"What the World Needs Now, Is ... "

Before anyone begins thinking "permissive" or "spare the rod, spoil the child," let me point out that I will be continually stressing how this development is not only a good thing (why wouldn't love be good?) but is one of the few sources of hope for our future we really do have.

For less childhood pain and trauma means one is stronger and more able to face the even deeper perinatal pain.

Choosing Lesser Evils

At any rate, the extreme acting-out and total dissociation from the perinatal exhibited by the World-War-Two Generation was followed, in the generations coming after, by less relative dissociation and less horrific forms of acting it out. Quite simply, generations as a whole had better ability to refrain from the more blatantly evil act outs — wholesale murders and world wars, pogroms and genocide, inquisitions and witch-burning, racism and slavery. They were more able to choose seemingly milder forms of suffering and self-destruction — polluting the atmosphere, water, and food; population explosions and crowding of cities; and traffic jams.

The common everyday traffic jam is especially instructive of perinatal dynamics as traffic congestions replicate asphalt birth tunnels where one not only breathes exhaust fumes from trucks and other autos — fetal malnutrition — but also can become gridlock at any moment, thus re-creating the intense frustration and no-exit hopelessness, and rage, of BPM II.

Baby-Boomer Perinatal Awareness

Other examples of the scenery of modern times where the perinatal is manifesting but is less projected onto another:

We Know THAT We Don't Know ... We Could Be Wrong.

Many baby-boomers had enough access to their perinatal underbellies to question the absolute rightness of the Vietnam War and so they campaigned against it. This is indicative of closeness to the perinatal because it shows an ability to doubt one's egocentric defenses — as given by society and family of origin — and to look at situations from the eyes of the Other.

So much was this evident in boomers that some were even able to see the Vietnam War through the eyes of the enemy — exemplified by Jane Fonda's trip to Hanoi, the waving of North Vietnamese flags at demonstrations, and the carrying of little red books of the sayings of Chairman Mao tse Tung.

But It's Clear *You're* Wrong.

The baby-boomer — or Sixties — generation also indicate their closeness to their perinatal in their campaigns against some of the act-outs of the perinatal mentioned above: These include actions against pollution; a rejection of city life, with its gridlocks, pollution, and crowding , and a return to the country, in communes or otherwise; an awareness and rejection of polluted foods and creation of a natural and organic foods movement; and actions against global overpopulation including support for birth control, a pro-choice stance on abortion, and delaying of baby-making on their own parts along with a reduction in the size of their families.

The sexual excess that is characteristic of the perinatal, specifically BPM III, was evident in boomers' free love and promiscuous sexual behavior.

Many more examples could be given. But the proof of their closeness to their unconscious dynamics lies not only in their actions — as mentioned above, in their more blatant acting them out or in their actual actions against the blatant acting out, both of which indicate closer access — but also in the study of their unconscious dynamics. As mentioned in Chapter Four, Kenneth Keniston found in his study of the psychodynamics of the Sixties generation when they were in their youth an unusual amount of perinatal symbolism and self-analysis. (See "Raging to Reenter, Digging Under Ground.")

Boomer Rage, Perinatally So

We Shall Overcome.

We also see perinatal feelings in the focus of the baby-boomers on *empowerment*. This word appears to come up in every area of their lives. It can be seen as the natural focus of a generation that feels itself inside to be a helpless fetus facing an overpowering obstruction of a womb.

Hence baby-boomers are of course also closer to the frustration, rebellion, and yes, rage, that is part of the perinatal complex. We saw it exhibited by them in their anger at authority in the Sixties, their rebellion against the Vietnam War.

"Get the &%$ OFF Me!"

Keep in mind that a huge aspect of the perinatal is feelings of restriction, thus frustration, and, consequently rage against large entities of obstruction — like the womb was in relation to the small and helpless fetus. In doing so, we see that the reason for their rage is simple and understandable.

Baby-boomers, characterized as being closer to their unconscious, especially the perinatal, have more access to their anger: This means they feel their anger and are less likely to act it out in more hidden, disguised, and dire ways such as war-making, racism, and anti-Semitism.

This does not mean their rage would not be troublesome. The perinatal lets no one get off scot free. We see lots of pre- and perinatal anger coming out in the last few decades in the phenomenon of the "angry electorate." Let's look at that next.

More recently these baby-boomers have been coming into the *triumphant phase* of their lives. They make up the largest sector of the electorate, and their influence is reflected more as they come into positions of power in the media and elsewhere.

The Angry Electorate and Boomers

But their influence has been diffused and confused because of the anger of some of them. Their irrational rage — combined with the reactionary consciousness of the Fifties Generation, many of the Fifties Gen children of Yuppies-Gen Xers, and the remaining WWII folks — has most often skewed election results against the Boomers interests and their true desires. Though not the majority of boomers, enough of them expressed their rage to swing election results in favor of the other side.

1992 — "Mad as Hell"

Beginning in the 1992 and 1994 national elections, these baby-boomers exhibited their perinatal influences in contributing to the totally unexpected phenomenon of the "angry electorate."

At the time, pundits and media analysts were at a total loss to explain the rage of the electorate that was affecting these elections. In 1992, they were totally surprised by the showing of three men in particular — Jerry Brown, Pat Buchanan, and Ross Perot — who seemed to have one thing in common: the angry tones and rebelliousness that characterized their speeches, as compared to others.[4]

The demeanor of these candidates was at such odds with the other candidates that when Bill Clinton one night responded angrily to a comment by Jerry Brown about Hillary, Clinton's wife, it was that part of the debate — of Clinton being angry, all issues aside — that made the news that night!

Though the rage of the electorate in 1992 caused the Brown, Perot, and Buchanan phenomena, it was split among them, so Clinton ended up winning. This of course was also OK with the baby-boomers in that (1) Clinton and Gore were baby-boomers like themselves and (2) in the race against Bush, Clinton was the challenger, and thus the rebel; and Bush was the "bum to be thrown out."

However, this rage did not go away after the election, which highlights its having perinatal origins. In fact, after the shortest "honeymoon period" in history, by some accounts, it became directed at the most likely target/center — the President, Bill Clinton, himself.

We all know how despite the successes and progress of Clinton's first year, he was especially singled out for ridicule and denigration by the media. He could not seem to do anything right, and the most incredibly outrageous behaviors were attributed to him.

1994 — "Throw the Bums Out … Again."

This rage spilled over into the next year and, sure enough, during the midterm election — the issues be damned — the angry electorate was in a mood to "throw the bums out" again. It did not matter the party … .I do not claim that all those of my generation are always as politically astute as they are angry.

The Republicans called it a "revolution." It was simply the acting out of an electorate in the throes of perinatal feelings — that is, feelings of frustration, being "tied up" by red tape, an inability to go forward … that is, up the economic ladder — wages had been stagnating since the early Eighties … being overcontrolled and pushed around by regulations … big government being the big mother womb keeping the fetus locked in and unable to move … and out of all this, the consequent anger and rage.

1996 and 1998 — "To Hell With You!"

At any rate, succeeding elections bear out this analysis of an angry electorate. In 1996, despite the much ballyhooed "Republican Revolution," sure enough, the electorate was spoiling to "throw the bums out" again — only this time it was the Republican Congress. So there were Democratic gains at the time.

And in 1998, when everything pointed to a huge Republican landslide because of the Lewinsky scandal, the electorate again showed their rebellion and anger toward both the pundits and the Republicans who had been lambasting them with details of the scandal for nearly a year by giving the Democrats gains again![4]

2006, 2008, and 2010 — Panicky Electorate

In 2006, 2008, and 2010, it was an angry electorate reeling against oppression; and in the case of 2010, doing it mindlessly, against their own interests. If there were not perinatal charge to all this, Americans would not be so irrational about their choices.

Perinatal Rage

People have had good reasons to feel oppressed since the Eighties when Reagan began the giveaways to the rich and the budget cutbacks, continuing to this day, that have caused the masses to feel constricted and oppressed.

Yet, if this did not result in their being perinatally overloaded so that they cannot reason, they would not have been able to be led to fight their own interests as they were in 2010 and in an ongoing way as exemplified by the Tea Party and the success of right-wing agendas.

Reacting, Too Angry and Confused to Think

Another aspect of this irrationality on both sides of the political spectrum has to do with this idea that there is no difference between the two major parties. Feeling oppressed perinatally is characterized by a pressure from all sides simultaneously. There is an inability to distinguish or discriminate between forces that are helpful and those that are dire, as any and all developments seem threatening in situations of crisis. In a situation of overwhelm, further, there is an inability to think clearly. One just fights back, explodes, reacts. It's no coincidence that righties are called reactionaries.

Biting the Feeding Hand

The upshot is an inability, under the pressure of perinatal feelings, provoked endlessly by actual oppression economically, environmentally, socially, and culturally, to rail against any authority, to bite the hand that feeds one. This is exactly like the panicked swimmer who in danger of drowning fights off his or her rescuer.

Can anyone at this point still maintain that the politics of the last few decades had anything at all to do with ideology or issues?

Right-Wing "Hate Groups," the Tea Party, and the Fifties Generation: Perinatally Oblivious

One might also note the rise of "hate groups" occurring at the same time as the phenomenon of the angry electorate. Hate groups fill their ranks from folks on the extreme right and their actions are exemplified in the Oklahoma bombing tragedy and more recently in the Tea Party.

Perinatally Clueless

But notice again then that these hate groups are always on the extreme right of the political spectrum and thus exemplify a World-War-Two mindset in relation to their perinatal unconscious: Specifically, the mindset is one of being completely cut off from one's unconscious dynamics and being in total denial of unconscious motivations so that one can have the complete certitude — lacking any access to the unconscious which would give rise to doubts — that makes violent actions possible.

However the reason for bringing up the hate groups is to show how much their actions as well are dominated by perinatal — in their case, totally unconscious — dynamics.

For without exception their reasons for rising up against the government — representing the overwhelming womb — has to do with frustrations, like the trapped fetus feels, in regards to "oppressive" taxes, governmental red tape, laws, and other regulations that they feel restrict their freedom ... to move freely, as one wanted to but couldn't, in the womb.

Tea Party and hate group ranks are prevalent with Fifties Generation folks. The Eisenhower Generation — after the WWII Gen and before Boomers — were born just before or during WWII. They are mired in prenatal fears coming from the fact that their parents were living through such distressing times as WWII and the Great Depression when they were inside their mothers. They were "marinated" in the womb with fear and insecurity. They also were not brought up with the societal advance in child-rearing the next generation of boomers, and those afterward, would be granted. So it is understandable they would be both cut off from perinatal access yet full of perinatal pushes and pulls to act out in confused and self-destructive ways.

Perinatal Access of Millennials

Being Boomer Kids, Wouldn't You Kind of Expect That?

Now on the other end of this perinatal spectrum we have the most recent generational cohort to be making a mark. The Millennial, or Baby-Boomer Echo generation, show the same inner access as their Boomer parents. They demonstrate as well their parents' consequent refusal to act it out on a larger scale: It has been said that the greatest concerns of those in this generation, now in their twenties and thirties, are the environment and racism-bigotry.

Activist, Progressive

They show the progressive bent of their parents, also, in their having a lot to do with giving America its first African-American president. And to the environment and minority rights, we need to add classism, economic fairness, and human rights because of their phenomenal outpouring of support in 2011 for Occupy Wall Street and for union rights in Wisconsin and other states. They are showing global strength in opposing fascism, economic injustice, political oppression, and human rights abuses in Occupy and Arab Spring movements. They've filled massive demonstrations against the draconian economic policies of Republicans in Wisconsin.

Climate Change and The Environment

We know how pollution and action against pollution indicates a closeness to one's perinatal. To put it another way, it is clear that only a total denial and disconnect between one's consciousness and one's unconscious perinatal dynamics would allow one to act it out unconsciously in the creation of pollution and in the denial of it as a problem or a mindless neglect of it. So the fact that these Baby-Boomer children, the Millennials, are so cognizant, concerned, and active in relation to global pollution and climate change shows their lack of denial of this perinatal act-out.

Multicultural, Resisting Racism and Oppression

But what of racism and bigotry? How is this an indication of a closeness to the perinatal. There are several ways in which this is so. As mentioned, a closeness to the perinatal allows one to doubt one's given defenses and to glimpse alternate perspectives — in particular to look at things from the eyes of The Other.

In this way, the baby-boomer echo generation are able to see oppression, injustice, and unfairness as it is played out in the lives of minorities who don't share their (predominantly) middle-class advantages. They simply don't "get" racism, sexism, or bigotry of any kind; it is incomprehensible to them. They strongly oppose imperialism, colonialism, or oppression of any kind. Relatedly, they support animal rights and oppose animal abuse and cruelty. They don not understand torture and violence against fellow planetmates.

Naturally they were helped in that awareness by the gains of previous decades, beginning in the Sixties, which had them growing up with diversity of racial and ethnic heritages — seeing things multiculturally not narrowly — in their schools and in the omnipresent media. They grew up with the environmental awareness that was set in motion in the Sixties; they do not know of a world before recycling and energy conservation. Activism, demonstrations, and political action have been a part of their lives since they were born, unlike the several generations that preceded them and even their Boomer parents who grew up in a politically castrated Fifties.

But there is another, stronger element. This is the factor of oppression and unfairness itself. We experience compression (oppression), and frustration at our attempts to go forward, and what feels like hopeless unfairness and injustice, when in the throes of BPM II birth trauma. To see these facets of the fates of minorities, as in racism, or gender or sexual bias, points to this echo generation's closeness to their own perinatal oppression; hence their ability to empathize with oppressed minorities.

This ability to realistically sense and respond to oppression is also the reason they would throw themselves in heartily in defense of unions, an increasingly oppressed middle class, and public sector employees.

A Hierarchy of Healing?

This idea that those close to their unconscious conflicts are more likely to act them out blatantly goes completely against one of deMause's tenets. He wrote, "The higher the psychogenic mode of the psychoclass, the less it is necessary for it to act out its conflicts."[5]

However this is exactly the crux of my difference with his theory and is a central point I am making. For, from my perspective, the higher the mode of child-caring equals the less the defenses. Hence, the more it is likely that that generation's conflicts will be close to the surface, seeking resolution … like Maslow's *hierarchy of needs* theory. We might want to call it a *hierarchy of healing* theory.[6]

In other words, our observing the supposed "acting out" of an underlying trauma does not mean that the group or person in question is actually or, at least completely, "acting it out" and defending against it. It may be that that group is resolving, healing, or integrating it — taking it inward rather than acting it out … in the world, on others … whether to a small or great extent. Using the analogy of Pandora's Jar, described earlier, they are opening the jar, at least a little. And I disagree with deMause in that I wish to stress that it is healthier by far to do that. Let me explain:

The difference between acting out and resolving is whether the actions are done in total dissociation from the unconscious dynamics, that is to say, in a trance state — as explained earlier in regard to the World War Two generation and the Tea Party — or whether there is at least a modicum of insight into it occurring as a result of things inside of oneself, not completely projected onto the outside.

The attitude that leads to total dissociation and acting out was expressed in the 2012 military movie, *Act of Valor*, which depicted Navy Seals engaged in anti-terrorism activity. At the end, the manner of dealing with pain recommended for these American soldiers and "men of valor" was to (paraphrasing) put all the pain in a box, shut it tight, press it down till it is smaller and smaller, and never, under any circumstances, let it out!

However, in non-acting-out — "acting inward" or taking back the projection — there is a tad of insight, as, for example, in the "overexamined life" of the "uncommitted" and the "self-analysis" of the young radicals of the Sixties generation. Similarly, the rock concert revivication of all current generations except the Fifties and WWII ones, as I've mentioned, is about personal experience and growth, and it is not about acting out on another; whereas an example of the extreme other end of that would be engaging, trance-like, in a mass killing against a perceived political enemy, as Loughner did in Arizona, and as we do as nations in wars.

Another example of complete dissociation is the anti-abortion folks. They do not have a clue of the connection between their own unconscious prenatal pain and the feelings they have about unborn others. They are not wrestling with their feelings, they are trying to change the world to conform to their defenses around those feelings — that is, they want the world to suppress that womb time out of existence like they have done to it in their own minds. The proof that it is acting out is that it is all about changing *others'* behavior, and it involves imposing one's inner pain on others forcefully and aggressively — which we have seen in its extreme form with the murders of physicians committed by anti-abortionists

Flaunting One's Sickness Beats Hiding It — Generation X

The self-analysis of the Sixties Generation was followed by a different mode of struggling with perinatal pain by Generation X, which continues in abated form with the Millennial Generation. It was manifest rather strikingly with the Goth phenomenon and the vampire fascination that began in the Eighties, coincident with Gen X's coming of age. Goth and vampirism show blatant perinatal dynamics that are not unfelt and completely repressed as in dissociation with its trance-state aggression against others. An example of Gen X perinatal acting out of these dynamics in total dissociation and trance state was given above in the anti-abortionists. But Goth and vampire culture show folks feeling and immersed consciously in these pushes and pulls and wrestling with them, trying to work them out as opposed to act them out.

Hey, It Was Tough!

This is rather clearly shown in looking at the "regression" in Europe, described by psychohistorians, which occurred in the Nineties. This behavior showed a bit of insight … and resolution happening … in that the baby song being hummed was about the very real hardships of being a baby. Therefore, an actual truth about their own lives was being faced there by those singing along with it. The song was not being used to deny or defend against those traumas.

One might suspect that as well in carrying around such blatant examples of regression as a pacifier. For someone in a more defended mode would be highly threatened by such an obvious symbol that they are really needy children inside. More defended folks would be terrified such overt behavior would make them look wussy or sissified — that is, look like that vulnerable, frightened baby that they really feel themselves to be but are doing their damnedest to hide from everyone. Imagine how those Navy Seals described above would feel walking around sucking on a pacifier, for example.

So in actually carrying around a pacifier these youth were not only displaying an insight into their feelings of sometimes being needy babies, on the inside, but are actually flaunting this awareness, as if to shame, or slap the face of, or be "in the face" of a generation of their parents — the Fifties Generation for the most part — who did not see their needs when they were babies — however effortfully and obviously they sought to demonstrate them. Thus the symbols needed to become more and more shocking and obvious.

Look at What You Did to Me!

For example: the jeans with requisite holes around the knees was screaming out, "You did not take care of me; you made me feel like a poor, orphaned, ragamuffin child."

The piercing of mouths, nose, ears, and even tongues shouted,

I am in pain, dammit! Can't you see that when you stick needles in me as a little baby that I hurt? How can you be so insensitive? Can't you see that when you refuse to breastfeed and thus nurture me orally that I am forever damaged there, ever painful there? What does it take, my sticking pins — safety pins make the point even more that it was when I was in diapers — in myself to make you see that I hurt there?

And, of course, the black clothes, the hideous macabre makeup, and depressed, sullen expressions was exclaiming,

Look, you might think we're a wonderful family and everything is hunky-dory here; but I wish I were dead! I've felt so much pain, from in the womb, at birth, and right after birth, that I wish I'd never been born.

Also, somehow in courting death, I have the feeling that I might somehow be reborn again into a good life, not like this place of torture and tears, right from the beginning, where my welcome into the world consisted of being drugged, handled like an object or piece of meat, blasted by bright lights, scrubbed by rough cloths, having needles and suctions stuck in me, blasted with noise, made to lie on cold stainless steel surfaces, and then bundled like a tamale so that I could not move ... making me feel again like I was back in the hellish womb where in the later stages, for a time that felt like an eternity, I felt unable to move and was suffocating for lack of sufficient oxygen ... and the only action that was possible was for me to scream my bloody head off for long periods of time or go into a stupor — which is what I did, alternating between them.

Can't you see that I'd rather be dead than live in such a world of insensitive zombies like you. Hell, in fact, to further drive the point home, I'll even look and act like a zombie, I'll try to appear as unfeeling and morose as you all seemed to me, especially at my birth. And I'll go a step further and mirror yourselves back to you by becoming enamored of vampires....

Can't you see that you sucked my very life force, my blood, and turned me into an unfeeling vampire like you, by suffocating me in the womb, poisoning me with your toxic blood which you both sucked from me and then forced down my throat!

Different Levels, Different Defenses

It is instructive at this time to note that Arthur Janov once compared the defenses that characterized the youth of the time — the late Sixties, early Seventies — with those of their parents and older people in general and came up with findings that amplify my own assertions here.

"Mind's Made Up, Don't Confuse Me With the Facts!"

Specifically, Janov found that older people — clients of his as well as others of whom he was aware — were characteristically more repressed, more split off, more prone to dissociation, more defended and, most importantly for our uses here, tended to use defenses of denial and obfuscation against inner information and impulses. Correspondingly, they tended to use drugs that repressed and blotted out reality, such as alcohol and nicotine; and they tended to be sexually repressed. They were also more compulsive. They tended to suppress their tension and hold it in for all their worth.

"How Can You Have Any Pudding if You Don't Eat Your Meat?"

Truth was greatly feared, and all attempts were made to fend off incoming information that might threaten the delusional reality set of the conscious mind. This left them open to the characterization: "My mind's made up! Don't confuse me with the facts!" which was leveled at them by anti-Vietnam War protesters. In more recent years, it is no wonder they have engaged in a war against education and against Hollywood, as really they are at war with new information. Consequently, Janov found that the dominant mode of reaction, when threatened, was to act out aggressively against the supposed "oppressor." Like prenates up against an overpowering womb, they are in constant war with overwhelm.

"Peace, Out."

On the other hand, he found that his youthful clients — under 30 — tended to use defenses of excess, release, and addiction, or to be unusually lacking in defense mechanisms. They were more impulsive. They tended to have weak barriers to incoming information, to be open to negative unconscious content, even at the expense of their self-esteem, and to be tension expressers. They were therefore more likely to be sexually promiscuous than repressed, and they tended to use drugs that opened them to information and unconscious knowledge — such as marijuana and LSD.

Consequently they were less split off from their unconscious truth … though it made them uncomfortable … were less repressed, and, if anything, used defenses of masochism, self-denial, and self-inflicted aggression or depression. Truth was more important to them than emotional comfort. They tended to go out of their way to dig up negative information about themselves, and they accepted the low self-esteem and sense of self-worth that came with that kind of openness to truth.

Their delusional reality set — if it could be called that — entailed taking on the worries and cares of the world as their own, since their openness to their own cares and worries allowed them to empathize with others in obviously similar situations. When triggered into their pain, their dominant reaction was to take it inward and to take it out on themselves causing depression. In doing so they showed they would rather hurt themselves than hurt another.

Generation Gaps ... Again

I don't believe you need to be a rocket scientist to see that Janov was discovering an historical — one might say millennial — "changing of the guard" as regards access to the unconscious, openness to personal truth, and lessening of the tendency to act out early trauma in violent or belligerent ways. The older generation had more tendencies to blame others, to find scapegoats for their ills, and to act out violently on them. The younger generation had more tendencies to look inward and to blame and punish themselves ... and to prefer to hurt themselves before hurting another. They would more likely cut themselves than cut another; they would more likely commit suicide than kill.

The youthful generation might also become alcoholic, addicted to drugs, or do something else to injure themselves ... rather than act it out on another.

Less Wars, More Suicides

And this "acting in," as opposed to acting out, is indicated as well in the rise of teen suicides in recent decades. So you might say that the tradeoff we are currently getting is a reduction in the use of wars and racism to solve problems — that is, a reduction in the tendency to act out one's Pain on others and to scapegoat. But, since the perinatal trauma is still there, and one is even more conscious of it, we have increased suicides. We have not had a world war or dropped a nuclear weapon on people since World War II; but we suffer unceasingly from relatively less loss of life in regional conflicts and the self-inflicted harm of air, water, and food contamination and from radiation poisoning from nuclear power plants. We have not had millions killed in genocides or purges since World War II, but we have suffered lesser loss of life in uprisings for democracy in China, Iran, Syria, Southeast Asia, and the Arab world. We have not had lynchings and racial riots have ceased, but we have suffered less lethal damage from culture and class wars, increased incarceration, creeping fascism, and struggles for economic justice.

Overall then, less death, more suffering. Less killing in wars, more suicides. Less large scale atrocities, more depression. On a collective level, we are taking our conflicts increasingly inward.

As deMause pointed out,

Those considered 'neurotic' in each age may often be a higher psychogenic mode than those considered 'normal,' only they must stand the anxiety of not sharing the group-fantasies of the age.[7]

Away From Hubris: Nature Balances HerSelf

In this part on healing crisis, we have seen how perinatal acting out can be of two kinds: totally unconscious and trance-like, or semi-conscious with at least some access. We have looked at how a progression to more access to one's perinatal underbellies has led to more acting in than acting out. We have seen how it has led to less violence and more depression.

Suffering Beats Dying.

At this point, one could make the point that the tradeoff is worth it:

That individuals suffering more emotional pain and trauma is preferable to the horrors of world war and nuclear or genocidal holocaust … put bluntly, suffering beats dying.

But we are still looking at the situation from the microcosmic scale. We are talking and acting here like we are the only ones on Earth that matter.

This is natural of course, in that this is always the way we have thought of things — that is to say, as if all things were to be considered around the concerns of humans. This is called *anthropocentrism* — a form of *species-centrism* — in which *Homo sapiens* is considered the reason for the existence of the rest of the Universe.

With the Universe as awesomely and unimaginably large as it is, one might wonder at our hubris in considering things in only this way — that is, from our perspective.

Likewise, with a mind-boggling number of species living or having lived on this planet alone — species numbering in the hundreds of millions, if not trillions — again one might question the validity of choosing the perspective of our species alone in making our analyses.

How 'Bout We Step Outside?

Yet this is the way we have always done it. And this is the way I have been slanting my perspective so far in this book.

But now let us do something radically different. Let us walk out of ourselves — figuratively speaking — and seek to stand upon that Archimedean point from which we might view the events currently transpiring.

From such an attempted non-species-centric viewpoint let us view this emerging perinatal unconscious as it is currently manifesting in humans. However tenuous our attempt, let us at least try such a new-paradigm viewpoint. For certainly all old-paradigm ones — containing all the hubris of anthropocentrism that they do — have failed in their attempts to save our species and indeed have contributed to such a likelihood.

Let us attempt to see through the eyes of Gaia, now — from the viewpoint of Earth itself — as we look at how the current *human* predicament may in fact be an example of Nature balancing HerSelf. With both perspectives in mind, we can have a complete picture. We will return then to look at where there is cause for hope, what we are doing wrong as well as where there are positive trends and forces at work, and how we might let go of the self-defeating and instead apply ourselves to fostering the forces of good going on in global consciousness and the globe itself.

CHAPTER 7

THROUGH GAIA'S EYES — NATURE BALANCES HERSELF

"Tinkle-Down" Economics

"This land is your land," they sing. Taking them at their word, my wife and I spent a year, in the early Nineties criss-crossing *our* land in a twenty-three-foot Prowler travel trailer, pulled by an old but ambitious Oldsmobile with way too little horsepower. Our idea was to attend conventions and trainings in our field before we had to be in Northern California, by September 1992, where I had accepted admission into a graduate program.[1]

So West and East, North and South we went — there was much to see ... all too much to be alarmed about. This was, after all, in 1991-1992, the final year of the Reagan-Bush era when Reagan's voodoo economics had played its course in distributing the wealth upward to the wealthy where it could be squandered on luxury items like yachts and overpriced objects of art and the trickle-down theory had shown itself to be a piss on the poor or, let us say, "tinkle-down" reality.

Correspondingly, the 1980s "party" was over. It left little money for government to do its job properly, though. The National Debt, after all, had nearly been quadrupled in this Reagan-Bush give-away to the rich. Budget cutbacks at all levels of government were in effect ... and these cutbacks were grossly evident in what we saw.

"Neutron-Bomb Turf"

Similarly, the suckers ... or coke-heads, or both ... who had bought into the false prosperity promised by the Robin-Hood-in-reverse fiscal policies of the Eighties, were now waking up from their mania with the hangover of ill-conceived schemes in ruins surrounding them. This was apparent in the places we traveled as well. All over Florida and Georgia, for example, we saw shopping centers looking half like ghost towns — evidence of recent bankruptcies or, my wife wondered, is it possible those spaces were never leased?

The only thing comparable in my experience I could think of was Springfield, Oregon, during the recession of the early Eighties. I remember well, while doing door-to-door anti-nuclear canvassing, how up to half the houses in a given neighborhood would be empty and unoccupied ... the continual frustration of nobody answering doorbells leaves an imprint, I suppose.... We used to call it "neutron bomb turf"; and it almost — but not quite — served as an excuse for not making "quota."

In Springfield, where the lumber industry was taking a beating because of the lack of new housing starts caused by the recession, people had moved out of town to look for work where it still existed.

But in the South in the early Nineties it was somehow different. My wife and I wondered if this plethora of vacancies had something to do with the S&L scandal: all those boondoggles ... all those poorly conceived investment projects gone belly up, leaving only haunted shells as evidence of that mania.

Budget Cutbacks

Rest Areas

Throughout the South, evidence of the cutbacks in services was everywhere. Too often we found rest areas along the highways so overcrowded we had to drive on for lack of parking. We saw tractor-trailers forced to park along exit routes, or side roads — anywhere there was space. Some rest areas had "two hour limit" signs — something else I had never come across — and others were closed down completely ... "for cleaning," allegedly.

I half expected to see truck wrecks littering the roadsides as I envisioned the plight of truckers pushing on in bleary-eyed exhaustion for lack of some place to pull over; or raising themselves up from a dead sleep, in a fog, with an alarm clock set to abide by the two-hour limit. I myself was rather dangerously dazed several times when, in the wee hours, we were forced to continue past eagerly anticipated rest areas that turned out to be barricaded or otherwise unavailable.

These imaginings of sleep-driving truckers barreling, obliviously, across medians and into oncoming traffic it turns out were premonitions, as a few years later they were proven to be horrifyingly correct. In 1998 to be exact, this problem became big enough to finally become a story in the mainstream media. Highway deaths, caused by a lack of places for sleepy truckers to park, were piling up in numbers too large to ignore any longer.

Of course, the media provided an alternative to fully acknowledging this truth — as they are wont to do — by laying alongside the actual facts a concocted theory that some trucking companies were at fault, for pressuring truckers to meet unreasonable deadlines for delivery. Regardless, scores of cars and other trucks had been involved in some of these accidents, including head-on collisions, with people dead and many injured.

But in '91-'92, these realities had not been statistically blatant enough to make the evening news and went unnoticed. However our U.S. Congress was not completely oblivious to such effects of its cutbacks. "America can no longer afford to maintain its infrastructure," they said in 1993 when they had the chance to appropriate money for ordinary maintenance. To get themselves off the hook, they dared to call these highway and infrastructure funds "pork barrel." And instead they wrote laws to crack down on the truck drivers and their employers for overtime driving ... now that's gonna find 'em a place to pull over!

Roads

In our travels we also found that roads were often bumpy and wavy — "these are supposed to be freeways," I mused," not side roads." The "deteriorating infrastructure of America," they called it.

Signs

Related to this, we found many roadways were not clearly marked and signs were out of date. In trustingly following them, we got lost a number of times. It seemed nobody cared out there; nobody was paying attention. I lost count of the number of side journeys and turnarounds we were forced to make. I don't remember ever — in my fifteen or so transcontinental adventures over twenty-three years — having so much trouble with signs.

Often we were forced to return to the point of departure from the true course, and I'd examine the sign that led us astray. "Yes, dammit, the sign does indicate to turn here for that route." I wondered if perhaps that was once the correct way but had since been changed without the sign being corrected.

Some Joke

And then I imagined all the other cars, of all those others who didn't just so happen to live in the area and be aware of this anomaly, traveling up that side road and turning back around again … almost as if that were part of the route — to make that kind of loop before proceeding.

I pictured a local watching these cars, one by one, turning around in the course of a day. "Check it out, Mabel," he'd chuckle. "We got another one." Or, "Strangers in town! Strangers in town!" It is something to behold … smacks of human futility and ridiculousness.

Some Loss

I thought of the gallons of gas wasted in this way … of the jobs in maintaining these services — to keep things in working order and correct — that no doubt were lost.

I thought also of the huge sums of money, now gone, that could have been spent this way — money which was wasted instead for weapons to fend off a Red Menace that turned out to be a straw man. I recalled with anger how the warhawks tried to take credit for the downfall of Communism by claiming it a victory for their weapons-production policies, how I never heard it pointed out that the fact that Communism collapsed from within indicates a tremendous waste of money and poor policy to think that we needed to prepare to fight it from without.

But the Pentagon was not the only "bottomless well" in the Eighties. I thought of all the money funneled into the coffers of the wealthy in the orgy of extravagance that we taxpayers got the bill for as the S&L scandal. I thought how that money could have been used not only for signs, for roads, for rest areas ... but also for all the pressing needs of our people, so neglected in the Reagan-Bush years.

So much for being the "wealthiest nation in the world."

State Parks

And then there was the situation in the state parks. More than once we were prevented from camping for a night. We arrived too late at a park and were unable to enter — an iron gate barring the driveway.

We found other evidence of cutbacks: a cutback in employees; areas roped off and blockaded, not to be used. My mind liked to break into a "This Land Is Your Land" melody when encountering such barriers and fences; the overall effect would be altogether depressing.

Overpopulation

All this of course in addition to the other signs of deterioration: pollution of the countryside, over-industrialization, wilderness areas turned stinking and worn by commercial interests.

On one occasion while hiking in a Florida park, once more due to a lack of signs we lost our way. During the inadvertent nine-mile hike back to our campsite, we saw signs ... at least there was money for these ... indicating how the dunes should not be walked on because the sea oats would be worn down and killed — resulting in sand drifting, blowing around, killing trees, and destroying campgrounds.

And indeed everywhere we walked it appeared as if thousands of people had stamped beneath the trees, so that even the space between them looked like trails. I began to speculate on just how many people there are on the planet. Clearly the basic problem was there were too damn many of us here!

How Far Astray

I began to consider how far we've gone astray from any meaningful or sustainable path for our species on this planet. I reflected on how the effects of the changes we've made — for example, the reduction of oxygen in the atmosphere that goes with the increase of carbon dioxide, known commonly as *the greenhouse effect* — how it's been discovered that these effects keep people close to their unconscious pain, closer to their unconscious in general.

It is as if we as part of Nature are also regulated by Nature, that the very effects of our overpopulation and our straying from a cooperative ecological niche for our species result in consequences that are inevitably going to bring us back into line ... *one way or the other!*

Going Inward

Knowing as I do that environmental pollution and lowered oxygen levels promote diseases, general illnesses, hay fevers, epidemics of allergies, and a general weakening of our immune system — all of which, since the Reagan Eighties, we are seeing in abundance — I realized that people are more and more being forced to go inward because they are less and less able to go outward in a healthy manner.

Chastened by the Environment We've Created

Another factor in this is that the deteriorating quality of air and the increasing levels of toxins that we ingest are also attacks on ego defenses, which has important yet previously unexplored implications.

As I said previously, both Stanislav Grof and Arthur Janov — and others as well, I am told — at one time used carbon dioxide to take people into a nonordinary state of consciousness where they would be more open to their repressed traumas, to their unconscious mind. They did this to help these people heal these traumas.

They found that slight increases in carbon dioxide inhalation invariably brought up primal pain and birth-trauma feelings — that is, repressed painful feelings from our experiences of birth and infancy that our ego defenses normally keep "safely" tucked away in our subconscious.

Consider for a moment what that means for those trapped in the pollution-ridden cities! Though keep in mind that increased carbon dioxide is an atmospheric problem that affects everyone on this globe. I recall a TV report when I lived in the air-chunk-city of Denver, Colorado, in 1978. At the time, Denver's air was rated as being the second worst in the country, behind Los Angeles, partly because the high altitude made for thinner air and thus higher percentages of toxins relative to normal air. Anyway, the TV report proclaimed how the number of hospital admissions for spouse abuse, child abuse, alcoholism, and related violence would soar on days when the air pollution index was high.

Air Pollution as a Psychedelic

Apparently, the reduction of oxygen in these situations acts similarly to a reduction of blood sugar or glucose to the brain, which results in an inhibition of the ego's defensive ability to keep out unwanted information. Coincidentally, research has shown that this same kind of reduction of glucose to the brain is instrumental in producing the effects of certain psychedelics, including mescaline and marijuana.

But this reduction in defenses is not experienced or understandable only by those who have experimented with psychedelics. In fact, in at least minor ways we have all experienced it.

The workings here are similar to those in the common experience of being more cranky; irritable; irrationally emotional; more prone to depression, anger, and tears; more excitable; and in general, closer to one's "shit," when one is tired, overworked, or just gotten up from a sound sleep. In these situations as well, the brain is inhibited — here because of fatigue — from being able to effectively fend off unwanted information, impulses, and emotions.

The evidence concerning heavy metal toxicity indicates that it, also, can have a similar effect at times on one's mental and emotional state.

Global Cabin Fever

Also, there is the experience of "cabin fever," which many people are familiar with. We like to think that simply the fact of being cooped up for a long period of time psychologically leads to wanting to break out and be free, to be irrational and highly prone to emotional outbreaks, and in the extreme to result in delusions and hallucinations. But obviously this is not the case or else these symptoms would be rampant in other situations where one is contained for a long period of time, and they are not. It turns out that there are biochemical reasons — not simply the fact of being cooped up — which account for cabin fever symptoms.

Consider that cabin fever describes a situation, most often, in which one lives in an environment that is insulated against cold winter weather — thus keeping out fresh air. And in which, very often, oxygen is further depleted by the burning of oxygen-consuming wood fires in fireplaces or woodstoves, or oxygen-consuming coal fires ... whatever. With this in mind one can easily understand that environment is going to be increasingly deficient in its oxygen level as time goes on. Add what we now know about lowered oxygen levels leading to lowered defenses and eruption of unconscious content, and we can see how such environments can lead to the symptoms that, combined, we call *cabin fever.*

When you consider that on a smaller scale, with the greenhouse effect, we are globally setting up the same conditions as that of cabin fever, we can see why there would be an emerging perinatal unconscious occurring.

With the entire world suffering a low-level cabin fever, it becomes even more understandable why there is the current fascination with escaping the Earth and setting up colonies on other planets and in other solar systems. This idea we see in science fiction scenarios of all kinds — consider the popularity of the *Star Trek* programs and movies. But I've also heard it coming out of the mouths of NASA spokespersons.

At NASA, they have considered building colonies on Mars! A multibillion dollar project — talk about high-cost housing! But this fascination and irrationality is understandable when you think of it as a symptom of a global cabin fever. Apparently, we not only wish to be break out and be free in traffic jams, we have magnified it to wanting to break free of our planet itself — as if Gaia, Mother Earth, were some confining, stifling Mother-womb that we needed to bust out of or die!

Of course, the other symptoms of cabin fever — being highly emotional, irrational, delusional, and prone to hallucinations — we have already discussed as being part of the furniture of our current global reality, so we need not go into them here.

Back to the Drawing Board for Our Species

But the consequences of all these factors taken together are inescapable: As we edge our way, in a myriad of ways, toward global destruction, we increasingly "sicken" ourselves both physically and emotionally/mentally in the process. And this "sickening" is one of an eruption of unconscious material that causes us to psychologically "return to the drawing board" and seek solutions — both inner and outer — to our misery.

Down Can Be Up

Specifically, I am saying that inhibited brain functioning — whether through oxygen depletion, heavy metal toxicity, or other environmental anomalies — has the effect of heightened "mind" functioning … in the sense, at least, of lowered ego and defensive functioning. Thus, in the same way that psychedelic substances can open us to repressed perspectives by inhibiting "brain" activity, these environmental changes can be helpful in the sense of opening us up to suppressed individual … and global/universal … truth.

Therefore this "sickening," this seeming decline or going down, can really be an "up" — in other words, it can be viewed as part of a necessary "negative" retreat for the purpose of bringing in new information and re-evaluation. And we may then create anew our more harmonious ecological role based upon this more accurate information.

Now, I am not espousing environmental poisoning as a technique of higher consciousness. But I am saying that apparently Nature … and we are part of Her … has ways of balancing HerSelf.

Death As An Ally

In this respect I might note that our co-habitation with the bomb and with environmental destruction is a spur to our growth of consciousness in a way akin to the traditional spiritual paths that speak of the catalyzing power of "having death as an ally." That is, that the realization of the imminent possibility of death, which is in truth our existential condition, has been known to act as a spur to taking life seriously, and spiritually, and to "waking up" in general.

"Pay Attention!"

The power of this spiritual attitude can be imagined by considering how one would live one's life if one constantly asked oneself: "If I knew I was going to die tomorrow ... or in an hour, or next minute, *et cetera* ... how would I live this day ... hour, minute ... before me?"

Indeed, a lot of the transformative power of near-death experiences is known to come from their ability to jog one into awakening to the fact of one's mortality — the precariousness of one's biological existence. In this light, we might view environmental damage on a global scale, then, as analogous to the bonk on the head from the stick of a Zen meditation teacher, telling us to "pay attention!"

The upshot of all this is that with this degradation of the external environment we are forced to go inward, to go back to the drawing board, so to speak, whether we want to or not. Illness in general and lowered oxygen levels in particular lead to a rising up of people's repressed emotional pain, and they force us to confront the roots of our motivations and patterns of cultural engagement as well as our social and relational styles.

Moratorium

This "turning inward" is the essential meaning of the "peace" symbol, when you think of it. The upside-down cross pointing downward in a circle has rightly been used to symbolize "moratorium" — in other words, a period of halting of action in the world because nothing worthwhile can result from the ways we are currently doing things, and a turning away from the external world and looking inside to reevaluate. It is as if Nature, completely unbeknownst to us, balances us, pushes us down to our deepest programming and back to our earliest "grids," individual by individual, and that this forces us to reassess our lives and causes us to create more meaningful lifestyles, more synergistic patterns.

So in a sense Nature's reaction to our misconduct is to cause us — by means of the psychological effects induced by the biochemical alterations that are the result of environmental changes — to create new social and cultural forms. We cannot help but do this. And collectively, cumulatively, it cannot help but result in massive cultural changes of one form or another.

Eden Arise — The More Natural Self

Many have proclaimed, in these strange days, that it is our Western estrangement from Mother Nature — our particular need to *control* — that is at the core of the threats to the end of life on this planet. In such a case, one needs to regain harmony with Nature and acquire a consciousness of *cooperation, not* control.

It's Cooperative Not Controlling

As Grof has claimed — and my personal experience attests — such a cooperative human nature is indeed our most fundamental human nature. In contrast to the "me versus them," aggressive, and competitive imprint that is derived from our traumatic and premature human births, this more fundamental human nature is the result of a more fundamental imprint of symbiosis with the Other, as was the case in the womb surround during the relatively blissful prenatal period. The relation of the fetus to the mother at that time is one of cooperation, all needs met, flow in < —— > flow out, and synergy of intents.

And when, as an adult, we reconnect with this more fundamental human nature, this more fundamental imprint, it manifests in us as a tendency toward that same kind of reciprocal relationship — cooperative, synergistic, and mutually beneficial. Only, as an adult, the Other with which this reciprocal relationship is had is Society and Nature. For these bear the same characteristics and relation to the adult as the womb did to the fetus.

Our More Fundamental Human Nature — Back to Eden

Furthermore, as Grof and I and many others have discovered, such a more positive human nature occurs naturally in a person when they have faced, re-experienced, and integrated their perinatal unconscious ... as opposed to what is usually done, which is, completely denying it, projecting it on a scapegoat or enemy and engaging in wars and social violence.

So it is the recovery of this sort of more fundamental human nature — one in which we are in cooperative and mutually beneficial relationship with Nature, all life on this planet, and other humans — that would remove us from the brink of extinction.

Looking Through Gaia's Eyes

When you think of it, when you consider that all of Nature — the whole planet, Gaia — is threatened by the actions of our species, and that that Nature would want to avoid this by balancing the elements that are currently skewed, it may be just the kind of global situation we see now around us that Nature would need to create in order to save "HerSelf." It's simple: We either change or die. Hey, why the long face!? If Gaia doesn't look out for HerSelf, who will?

Acting Out

Granted, some people are not dealing in a healthy or positive way with the material that is arising. Instead of re-doing their basic programming, these people "act out." Thus we have increased crime, aggression, hostility, one person against another.

And this fact is glaringly apparent in our big cities, where many who are not integrating this emerging information from outside their ego boundaries — from the unconscious — sadly are instead venting the energy of their pain — which our degenerating environment is opening up to them or giving them access to — in violent, destructive, wasteful, self-destructive, and pathetic ways.

One can also look to the grasping at racism, nationalism, and fundamentalism, which are not primarily urban phenomena by any means. These conduits of hatefulness are also a response that people are using to the feelings of pain, uncertainty, insecurity, and doubt that rise up, especially initially, in conjunction with these emerging truths.

Similarly, a great majority of people in general in our society are using drugs of one form or other to gloss over and obscure this emerging material rather than facing and integrating it. All in all these kinds of responses add up to a tragedy. And it is something that, if these reactions end up prevailing, could actually do every one of us in.

Helping Out

But about these others, what can we do — those of us who *are* changing our programming and creating new cultural patterns? It may be practical and advisable much of the time to just get out of their way if the ones acting out choose to kill each other off.

But we are often not able to "get out of the way" of those who are trapped in negativity. In addition, since we are all interconnected, we are bound to at least be indirectly affected by their actions.

And most importantly, since we are One and these others are actually ourselves in different garb, to the extent we are able to show compassion and be of assistance, we should not always want to step aside. I begin taking this up in the next chapter, "Derailing the Cycles of War and Violence." I discuss more fully how exactly we can be helpful to these others, in both small and large ways.

"Eve of Destruction" or Scenery of Healing?

To put the current chapter's theme another way: If we were to concoct a world situation in which we would be forced to take a quantum step in consciousness evolution by healing the nefarious elements of our perinatal unconscious, would not that world situation look something like what we see around us today? Would it not be a world rife with obvious perinatal elements ... and influences ... with some people resolving and thus being healed of them? While others would act them out and self-destruct because of them ... not to mention contributing to our collective global self-destruction, as mentioned earlier?

In other words, the situation today, as it looks, could as easily be seen as a prologue to an apocalypse and just as easily be seen as a healing crisis preceding a massive consciousness transformation. Put another way, this same situation can be seen by one person as the "eve of destruction" and another as the "scenery of healing on the pathway to peace." So which will it be?

In the next and final chapters of this book we will take a look at what are the most likely possibilities for ourselves and our planet, considering all that has been said so far. We will bring together all that we now know to conjecture: Apocalypse? Or Earth rebirth?

PART THREE

APOCALYPSE OR EARTH REBIRTH

CHAPTER 8

DERAILING THE CYCLES OF WAR AND VIOLENCE

The question posed at the end of the last chapter was whether we had opened the door to an unimaginable armageddon or were experiencing the birth pangs of a massive consciousness transformation and subsequent Earth rebirth. Are we going to self-destruct, bringing death to the entire planet along with us, or will we become good citizens of this planet and our species continue on?

What Say We Leave a Planet For Our Offspring?

Most folks would think there would be only one answer to that question desired by virtually all humans. But in other places, especially the chapter in the book that precedes this one in my Return to Grace series, *Apocalypse Emergency*, "Chapter Five: Thanatos Walking and The Only Question," I showed how, and why, that common-sense notion would, amazingly, be wrong: We saw how there is a huge percentage of our human Earth citizens, and a part of all of us, that wants to "throw in the towel." This has always been true of humans, but it is of critical importance only now.

But I will assume anyone reading these words will at least consciously be wanting our vital question to be answered in the affirmative. You know as well as I that the folks on the other side of this question are doing vastly different things right now than us and are nowhere to be found around here.

How Do We "Like" Life?

So the next thing to be addressed is how we might change our fortunes and live. Since continuing on is not just a matter of deciding it — voting "like" on it or checking its box — how can we get around this part of ourselves and our population that wants to do us all in? We need to know how to derail our perpetual cycles of war and violence. We need know how to quit bringing pollution and suffering on us. We have to know how we can stop our secret desire to take comfort in failure, how to "unlike" self-sabotage on our inner "profile."

How Do We "Unlike" Fascism?

I have written a great deal on this question, including an entire book in 2011 on the way we act out this masochistic tendency politically and culturally by taking comfort in totalitarianism and embracing fascism.[1]

For our purposes presently I will focus on the element of it all that is critical to answering our question. So we first need to look into the place from which emanates our dilemma. I showed that this bugaboo is our Will to Death.

Our Coming Into This World Makes Us Want to Leave It

Now we need to get more specific on this negative inclination of ours. As we have seen this Will to Death arises from human's unique-among-all-species primal pain rooted in our singular way of coming into the world — our unique human birth.

We Need Look Deeper

We need to look deeper into the elements of that part of ourselves that would have us take us all down. We need inquire into that tendency of ours to choose pollution over health, tyranny over freedom, war over peace, enslavement over autonomy, violence over pacifism, oppression over liberty, misery over happiness. We must derail the cycles of war, violence, and fascism. We must know how to "like" happiness.

We Need Know Where Exactly to Focus Our Efforts to Be Successful

To do so, we must separate the skeins of this inner entanglement and shed light into this darkness within. We need to know specifically, precisely where to place the lever of effort we will apply to truly move the world, to derail it from its current acceleration into oblivion.

So we look now into the elements of that perinatal unconscious manifesting currently as a will to die on the grandest scale imaginable.

Cycles of War, Cycles of Birth

We find there are two researchers who are particularly relevant to our understanding of the elements of the perinatal unconscious in a way as to avert collective, worldwide disaster. These are Stanislav Grof and Lloyd DeMause.[2]

Men Would Rather Be "Manly" Than ... Alive ...

DeMause writes,

The group-fantasy shared prior to wars expresses the nation's deep feeling that the increase in pleasure brought about by the prosperity and progress that usually precede wars "pollutes" the national blood-stream with sinful excess, making men "soft" and feminine" — a frightful condition that can only be cleansed by a blood-shedding purification.[2]

Men are more terrified of appearing "feminine" than of losing their lives. Why we invite war.

DeMause is saying we go forever into war because after a while peace makes men feel guilty, "sinful." Men have uncomfortable, even shameful ... homophobic ... feelings of being "soft" or "feminine" when their lives are good. So men choose the "purifying," masculinizing ritual of war to fight off these feelings. Nothing distracts one from looking inward better than a "good, old-fashioned" life-or-death struggle, and war is the most all-encompassing of them.

Men are more terrified of appearing "soft" than having the boot of totalitarianism on their neck. Why we allow fascism.

What deMause says about bringing war upon us can be said also about allowing fascism, inviting totalitarianism. For whether we are fighting enemies of another nation or struggling to survive against oppression at home, we are involved in a daily struggle. Secret to us, we feel better being engaged in a dramatic battle, though it brings us suffering and misery.

We simply can't hack peace for very long. We feel guilty, for some reason, lolling on the beach. You ever notice how at the end of your vacation time, you are anxious for it to be over and to get back to work? That feeling — that one where we feel ... guilty? ... uncomfortable ... tense? ... unfulfilled? ... (you tell me) — that's it. That's the one I'm talking about.

It happens the same way collectively after we have experienced a "vacation" of national peace — for example, in the Nineties when we were prosperous and mostly peaceful under Clinton. At the end of it, with George W. Bush, we ended up getting the misery and struggle many in America were driven to want, though no one would ever admit that.

A quick aside. The fact that the majority of Americans actually *didn't* vote for Bush and so tried to choose happiness over struggle is a source of hope for us in all this. That's a hint of what is coming.

Four Kinds of Experiences in Our First Nine Months Imprint Us for Four Feeling "Flavors" as Adults

But for now, let us get back to this opening provided us. We can make better use of deMause's insight on the birth feelings that take us into war using Stanislav Grof's delineation of this birth unconscious of ours. Let us review as described earlier and further stipulate on them: Grof explains we are moved as adults by four specific kinds of drives emanating from our earliest experiences. These specific tendencies in us relate to four different times in the birth process which involve four radically different kinds of experiences.

Grof uses the term, *basic perinatal matrices* (BPMs), to refer to these four aspects of our inner urges. I will describe them here and refer to them along with DeMause's cycles of social-historical violence and war to pull apart the roots of our current apocalyptic dilemma.[3]

Our Tendency to Always Screw Up a Good Thing, BPM I

The first of Grof's aspects of our unconscious he terms *Basic Perinatal Matrix I, BPM I* for short.

Prosperity and Progress Equal Feeling "Soft" and "Feminine"

Grof's BPM I is sometimes described as "oceanic bliss" and involves the experiences and feelings related to the relatively undisturbed prenatal period. On the social, macrocosmic level, it is the period described in the quote by deMause above in which there is a period of "prosperity and progress" and feelings of being "soft" and "feminine."

The strong connection between individual experience (personal psychology) and collective realities (social-historical events and elements) is patent here since in BPM I experience the individual is still in the mother's womb and to some extent shares her identity, which is of course feminine. Being unborn and not having gone through the "toughening" experiences of birth and later trauma, which predominantly create one's defenses, the individual is also "soft," in other words, undefended.

"No Pain, No Gain," Hell, Satan, and Poisonous Placenta; BPM II

"No-Exit" Claustrophobia

To further review Grof's schema and its relation to deMause's cycles of war, I want to remind you that BPM II is related on the individual level to the time near the end of pregnancy when the fetus is no longer rocking blissfully on the waves of oceanic bliss but is trapped in an ever more confining womb. As the fetus grows in size, the suffering becomes greater; no doubt this is the source of the common-sense belief that growing has to involve suffering, for example, "No pain, no gain." At any rate, the feelings are those of claustrophobia and "no exit."

There is heavy non-agitated depression here, since there appears to be no hope, no change in the situation that would indicate a way out of the suffering. Indeed, this period continues practically right up to the time of birth, ending only when the cervix becomes dilated and, experientially speaking, there appears suddenly to be a "light at the end of the tunnel" and therefore, hope.

Where the Hell We Get the Idea of Hell

However, up until that time there are feelings of being totally unempowered, completely in the hands of an entity — the womb — that imposes a horrifying reality that appears to be unending and eternal. Herein we have the psychological roots of notions of hell and Satan. Feelings associated with this state include despair, victimization, blame, and guilt.

"You'll Wallow in Your Shit, and You'll Think You're Happy." — Kurt Cobain, from the Song, "Sad"

As birth comes nearer, "fetal malnutrition" increases, since the neonate's increasing size and weight press down on and constrict the blood vessels that carry blood to and from the placenta, when the mother is standing. The decreased blood supply means a reduction of life-giving oxygen as well as the buildup of toxins that would otherwise be taken away by a normal blood flow. So feelings of suffocation as well as skin irritation and other feelings of wallowing in waste matter — deemed *poisonous placenta* by deMause — increase.[4]

"You're Really in a Laundry Room." — Kurt Cobain, from the Song, "Sad"

As I have said previously, deMause has found that these feelings exist to an extraordinary degree in a society and its leaders prior to its engaging in a war. Similarly, they precede, and obviously can be held to be accountable for, individual acts of violence — including everything from murder and rape to unfortunately all-too-common and ordinary spousal and child abuse in the household, and of course everything in between.

Bloody War, Bloody Birth — BPM III

BPM III is birth. Its social analogue is war or violent assault. Feelings that accompany this state on both the individual and societal level include rage and intense aggressiveness, all-encompassing struggle, and sexual excess.

Nothing's Ever Good Enough, BPM IV

BPM IV relates to the time of actually coming out of the womb and the post-natal period. On the societal level it is the ending of a war.

"Busting Out All Over"

Feelings of expansiveness, release, exultation, coming finally out into the light and/or being "on top" of things, and victory are feelings associated with this matrix, whether in the individual birth or the collective war cycle.

As I said the societal analogue to BPM IV, or actually being born, is a war's end. It is no coincidence that in triumph or peace, the two-finger peace symbol is used. What better way to signal we have come from constriction into openness, specifically through the vise of a mother's cervix, out from between two legs. As John Lennon so aptly put it, using the peace sign frequently, "War is over (if we want it)."

Mission Accomplished ... Not!

Interestingly, just as in recent times harsh modern obstetrical practices and the removal of the baby from the mother can leave lifetime feelings of success not bringing with it the expected rewards and thus a post-accomplishment sort of depression, so also the ending of successful wars sometimes also leaves a society with a sort of letdown. For example, the euphoria following George H. W. Bush's Gulf War — which catapulted his approval ratings into the ninety percent range in 1991 — was followed, only a year later, by the increasing agony of a recession and Bush's defeat at the polls.

Cycles of Birth, Cycles of War

All of this is to say that in society, as in the womb, a period of uninterrupted and relatively undisturbed feelings of growth leads to feelings of depression — being too "soft" and "feminine," but also "too fat" in the womb and, therefore, extremely constricted and compressed.

Why Women Fear Becoming Fat and Men Fear Appearing "Feminine"

Another way of saying this: feelings of expansion are followed by a fear of entrapment. And I agree wholeheartedly with deMause in saying that it happens this way in a nation's cycle of feelings because it happened that way to us prior to and during our births. We have these patterns of feelings as collective groups of individuals because our first experience of expansion was followed by extreme depression, guilt, despair, and then struggle and something bloodily akin to war — our actual births.

What Can Be Done?

So knowing this, how can we use it? In previous chapters, I explained how and why we see the dynamics of this perinatal unconscious, not coincidentally right now, on the ascendance, just at the time when it is crucial we deal with it to survive. I called this an *emerging perinatal unconscious,* and I went into detail about why it is happening now, what it means, and how we should take advantage of the opportunity it brings that could aid us in our current dilemma.

For now, I need only remind that it is imperative we face these unconscious forces instead of turning away from and thereby insuring our continued ignorance of them and helpless acting out of them.

So, how *do* we consciously participate in these drives, not merely be driven by them?

Lloyd DeMause, in his article, "Restaging of Early Traumas in War and Social Violence," printed in the spring 1996 issue of *The Journal of Psychohistory*, called for kinder and gentler birthing and child-caring practices to mitigate the ferocity of these forces within humans and help us avoid an otherwise inevitable planetary disaster. He was restating what other pre- and perinatal psychologists ... I am one, by the way ... including Thomas Verny and Stanislav Grof assert.[5]

However, I believe we need to go further than that. I, along with Grof, call for a larger awareness of and efforts in the direction of healing these perinatal elements in the consciousness and unconscious of those already alive right now. For unless we act to heal the people currently inhabiting this planet, we might not leave a planet that babies can be born into! ... let alone people to conceive and give birth to them. Healing the perinatal traumas can be accomplished through, at this point, thoroughly tested and effective techniques of experiential regression and emotional release.

But it is impossible for everyone to take advantage of these techniques, especially in the short time we have to make the changes. But something short of that ideal may be sufficient to stave off otherwise inevitable doom.

Let me explain what I mean by that.

Finding the Weakest Spot

Of course only time will tell what will be the result of this emerging perinatal unconscious for our species.

Real, not blindly delusional, action is required.

But to get an idea of what we might hope for, given a readiness to actually do something about this, I offer a perspective. This understanding requires we remember some critical aspects of the cartography of the psyche described above. Looking into them we might begin to see where are the openings allowing for realistic action to be taken to bring about true, not just blindly delusional, change for our species.

We can no longer afford otherwise.

For our purposes here, the most important part of the cycle is BPM I. Societies, according to deMause, go through these cycles of war and peace and have been doing so for as long as we know. But we can no longer afford these wars, as World War I and World War II have shown — with each one being an increase in our ability to destroy and to commit atrocities. We cannot afford to have a World War III as that most likely would end life on our planet.

Indeed, as I have been pointing out, we cannot even afford the less extreme forms of acting out of perinatal trauma that we have been doing in our poisoning of the earth and air, global overpopulation, and the ongoing regional wars to give just a few of many examples I could have used. These things, along with many other current quite insane tendencies of ours, have the capacity to end our species and possibly all life on this planet.

Feeling Good Is Not Bad

So the cycle of societal perinatal acting out must be stopped. And the most obvious place to derail the insidious cycle is at the point of societal prosperity and progress. Feeling soft, undefended, and feminine are, rationally speaking, not things to be alarmed about.

Quite to the contrary, it is rational that prosperity should make people feel good. It is rational that feeling soft should be a source of contentment, sensitivity, and intimacy with others. It makes sense that men should have no shame about feeling feminine because that only means that they have access to sensitive and nurturing feelings that are a source of joy, "color," and fulfillment in life.

Changing the Patterns of Millennia

But how do we do this? How do we convince people that feeling good is not bad? For these unconscious forces, these cycles of violence, have been pulling our strings for at least tens of thousands of years. How can we change such an engrained pattern?

Chasing the Mirages of the Future

Well, again, we get our leads from the experiences of individuals undergoing experiential psychotherapy.

"It's never enough."

For individuals also, if they are to heal themselves, have to learn how to appreciate success and to stop sabotaging themselves in the myriad of ways they do. Individuals act out their mini-cycles of "war" in their struggles to achieve. And people are driven to struggle to achieve because they cannot be pleased with what they have.

Relating back to deMause's societal schema, people cannot simply enjoy their "prosperity." People cannot stop to smell the roses occasionally. We cannot count our blessings and feel contented with what we have. Nor can we enjoy the natural pleasure of being alive in the moment.

"Wrong ... It IS enough."

No, instead what characterizes us humans — for the most part because of our having birth trauma — is a persistent drive to always have more than we do. We find that every accomplishment or success is short lived, with inexplicable depression following it. For each new attainment does not bring the expected (unconscious) rewards and leads us almost immediately to a new struggle, a new accomplishment to be sought.

Humans are driven to chasing mirages of better times somewhere off in the future, and we fail to live in the present. We feel unsatisfied with what we have and are continually deluded that some new possession, accomplishment, or love "conquest" will bring with it the missing happiness.

Becoming Self-Actualizing Instead of Self-Sabotaging

When people are aware of the way they unconsciously sabotage their happiness, they sometimes seek help. And if they seek help in the experiential psychotherapies, they are enabled to work through their birth trauma so that they are no longer driven out of the moment, with its pleasure and pain, into an imagined but never attainable pleasureful and happy future.

Learning that it is enough

So people derail their cycles of drivenness and their tendencies to sabotage their successes by learning to enjoy their "prosperity," even if it is the simple pleasure of being alive. And when they act to add to that pleasantness, they do so, not out of drivenness, but out of feelings of flow and the simple joys of acting and actualizing one's tendencies, talents, and desires. They become self-actualizing instead of self-sabotaging.

OK, knowing this, one might ask if I am suggesting that to save our species everyone needs to get into experiential therapy. While that would be nice, it is not practical.

But I believe it is not necessary either. There is an element of that societal period of prosperity that can be used and focused on in order to make the societal change of pattern, the societal derailing of the tendency to self-sabotage through war-making.

Getting By, With a Little Help From Our Nature

And that element is this: During times of prosperity, when one is less engaged in a struggle to survive, we find that one's body will naturally try to heal itself of unresolved and somatically imprinted trauma by bringing into consciousness the repressed traumatic memories needing resolution.

Hierarchy of Healing

This occurs in a manner similar to that of Maslow's hierarchy of needs. Basically, one's needs to "grow emotionally" … that is to say, clear away the unresolved trauma … can only come to the fore when one's physical survival needs are relatively taken care of. And arise they unerringly do, given any opportunity to do so.

"Don't Just So Something, STAND There!"

However, when these traumatic memories come up seeking resolution, they, also unerringly, bring with them the associated feelings of depression, unease, and pain. But because these feelings are anything but pleasant, to their detriment most people seek to avoid these feelings through addictions and other forms of "acting-out" behavior. So addictions and acting-out behavior emerge after periods of relative stability precisely because that stability allows unresolved feelings an opening for emergence and a possibility of resolution and healing.

Allowing Our Society to Be Honestly, Blatantly "Sick"

So there you have it; that is the crux. The period of societal prosperity can be maintained and added to if that society refuses to run away from the negative feelings that come up with success. As I have said, one needs to get "sicker" in order to get really well.

"Stand in the Place Where You Are … Just Stand."

Societally, we need to allow the social, formerly repressed, "sicknesses," negativities, and the pain that comes with them to arise and be socially worked out, to be hashed out, rather than to escape them by resorting to scapegoating enemies and waging war against them.[6]

Are We Doing This?

But can societies do this? Are they doing this?

Apparently Not

It does not seem so at the moment. For we have extreme acting out going on from Tea Party type elements. The homophobia that characterizes them is an indicator of the degree to which they are fearful of that feeling of being "soft" and "feminine," I mentioned.

But Then Again ...

However there is a pattern in change that things cannot *really* change until the negative slide has "hit bottom." These negative forces cannot be gone beyond until they have wasted themselves in desperate acts. At this time also, positive forces are strengthening in the wings, burnishing their skills, tempering their character and nobility, fully capable when the time comes to take over. There are so many examples of this in social and individual histories, but not to get bogged down, I will mention one powerful one — Nelson Mandela. You can take it from there.

The more common thing to mention about change is that prior to a major paradigm shift, the forces on the decline *always* wage a fierce, *desperate* battle ... a bloody retreat, a burning of the fields, nearly suicidal and totally reckless forays.

We see people do this, too, just before they are about to change. We see people who self-destruct being the ones whose last desperate battle before awareness can dawn being something that takes their life and perhaps others with them.

We currently can point to Gaddafi, Assad, and other tyrants. We can observe reckless tea-baggers willing, as in the debt ceiling clash, to bring down the country for ideals that, however rationalized and spun, are at their roots as simple and crude as jealousy — of those smarter and more capable; hatred — of minorities, the poor, the "dirty," the "slobs," the "lazy" ... basically all the scapegoats society allows them to vent the rage of their inner fears and hurt on; and homophobia — that fear of being "soft," feminine, unmasculine, and being willing to kill or be killed rather than to let oneself be seen that way.

Homophobes Don't Fear Homosexuals ... They Fear What's Inside Themselves

Before continuing, one big misconception around that last point needs clearing up: *Homophobia* is at base not fear/hatred of homosexuals, it is terror/hatred of the "feminine" and "softness" inside of the man himself who is homophobic. And this is the result of tens of thousands of years of "civilization," still continuing, in which men are threatened with disapproval, ostracism, ridicule, attack, or worse for not repressing their softer sides down to the level of the norm of their group.

Boys Learn They Must Be Less Alive to Survive

Boys learn they must constrict their potentials and diminish themselves to that which coincides with — and does not threaten — the older males in their group or face severe punishment. Boys learn the consequences for not becoming less than they could be are severe, often from their own fathers.

Girls Learn They Must Feel Less Pleasure to Be Liked

And by the way, something similar goes on with young girls and the reduction of their potentials. We see a blatant example of this in the practice of *cliterectomy* — also called *female genital mutilation* — in some cultures. In this practice the older women —

mother and aunts usually — are responsible for this brutal and extremely painful and bloody attack. It tells little girls they will have no pleasure more than that which was allowed the older women, themselves, in that patriarchal world. So girls must diminish themselves in order to not be hated and ostracized by the women of the group, who, already having been diminished, would be jealous of someone being allowed to have what they have not. This is an exact mirror image of the process that goes on in the diminution of the personalities — the potentials — of young boys.

A Hard Rain's Gonna Fall

Now to continue: So seeing so much of this pathos, hate, and bitter fear and anger is hopeful for us to be near the end of the cycle. Certainly it could get worse. But I personally do not see how we could go much further on this path to oblivion without going past the point of no return. Perhaps we are not meant to succeed. Perhaps we are doomed. But I know in my own life, and that is the only true basis anyone can have for knowing how things really work, that, without fail, every seeming "loss of ground" was a prelude to an even bigger "advance."

As Jung said, we need to take two steps backward to make a big leap forward. That is the way individuals are. And societies and populations are just collections of individuals. As the Tao symbol depicts, the seed of light is in the depths of darkness. So we can hold on to that, for one thing.

So Let Us See. A Scenery of Healing?

With these considerations in mind, the next chapter will evaluate our current social-cultural scenery for our prospects. In "Regressions in the Service of Society — Messy Healing," we will look for any indications that this standing firm in the face of the rising up of the repressed social Shadow — allowing the pain of it and facing it foursquare, hashing it out — is to be found in the current social arena.

If we can find this being done, we may allow ourselves at least the hope for a change in consciousness radical enough to save us from extinction. On the contrary, if we find little or no evidence for this kind of auspicious, fruitful healing activity, we might as well consider ourselves doomed.

CHAPTER 9

REGRESSIONS IN THE SERVICE OF SOCIETY — MESSY HEALING

Wedded to Rebirthing Rituals

At the point when the perinatal unconscious arises, individuals — and collectively, society — have the choice to turn toward the emergence of these feelings or to turn away from them.

In turning toward these feelings we embrace, feel, and if we go deeply enough into that, we relive the roots of them and resolve them finally.

In turning away from them we shun them, act them out, and are enslaved by them ... thus we act unconsciously, trance-like, zombie-like.

If we face these inner forces — we call that *feeling* them … in this instance, feeling through or reliving one's birth — we integrate them and heal the underlying trauma, the perinatal trauma.

Or the individual and society can avoid this going within — as depicted in the peace symbol — and can choose instead to act them out, which is the peace symbol upside down — the Satan symbol, the pentagram.

In acting them out, one distracts oneself from the uncomfortable feelings, which though not focused on, are still there. One tries to be "strong" in the face of feelings but one is actually driven and directed by them — they "take over one's mind." This is the source of the idea of spirit possession and in general of the idea that a devil or Satan can take over one's soul.

So in running from our feelings we are captured and enslaved by them, we are forced to act them out in ways we would not otherwise choose which are negative to horrible but in all cases self-sabotaging. Of course war is the most horrible, most self-sabotaging, greatest, and most all-consuming form of such acting-out … the greatest struggle.

Humans are characterized by a particular kind of birth process. It is a coming into being that is traumatic and which is related to our distinction of standing upright and thereby decreasing the pelvic opening as well as suffocating the fetus prior to birth. The fact is that because of this "distinction" we are destined to go through periods of rebirthing purificatory rituals, whether for good or ill.[1]

For we are psychologically wedded to reliving that which we could not fully experience at the time because of the overwhelming quality of pain associated with it.

A "Spiral Dance"

These rebirthing rituals we are doomed to repeat, one way or the other. We are going to act out this primal pain — this birth trauma — in an unending cycle of feelings having these components

- Periods of feelings of expansion
- Closedness or entrapment, guilt, and depression
- Aggression
- Release

Then back around again.

In winning the "war" or having the success or achievement, there begins the same cycle of expansion followed by entrapment. Losing the war ... the struggle, the battle ... is akin to death, even if there is no death. There is numbness and repression ... akin to a kind of "limbo" ... before life can begin anew. A reconception is necessary.

The Pattern of Our First Nine Months Imprints Us For Our Entire Human Lives

The reemergence of hope in individuals and societies is biologically equivalent to conception. And following this reconceiving, there is a similar cycle of reemerging strength — akin to the expansion that follows winning. Then there is continuing depression or overarching gloom and helplessness feelings coupled with revenge feelings and blame as individuals and societies stew in the vessel of indecision, inaction, and doubt. This is quite like the closedness and guilt which follows achievement-success-victory. Note, however, that the revenge and blame feelings here are aspects of the BPM II matrix, just as is closedness and guilt.

Can't Get No Satisfaction

And then the cycle is the same again. Specifically, there is aggression against the oppressor (War and revolution both see the foe as an oppressor, even if one is actually the one who is the aggressor.) What follows upon fighting is release or "death"; and so on around. The "happily ever after" that inspires such battle truly only exists in fantasies and fairy tales. Prosperity and feelings of success are unfortunately doomed, on this physical plane of existence, to be short-lived.

Where There Is Real Hope

It would seem we are fated to never be happy, for long. But progress is possible; herein lies our only real choice in the entire scenario. For we either work through these cycles in some deep psychologically transformative way that helps us deal with and pass beyond the difficult and painful parts of the cycle as well as helps to fade the imprints' potency in determining our behavior, or we are doomed to act them out in the external world in ways that we are blindly unaware are not congruent with the actual facts of our circumstances and are harmful to ourselves and others around us.

We are fated to experience these cycles of birth, and we will either act them out disastrously or find ways of dealing with them inside of ourselves in some way — and some ways are better than others for doing this — so that we can have some inner distance from these patterns and therefore some conscious ability or choice around our actions when these pushes and pulls arise.

The Vanity of Will, The Impotence of "Reason"

What we absolutely don't have, yet arrogantly think we do, is the ability — through will or reason alone — to choose light over darkness, to replace these inner veils of distortion with clarity of thought and perception and hence of positive behavior and actions while in the midst of them. Trying to reason with and to obtain truly desired outcomes is about as possible as trying to reason with a lizard and convince it to conform to one's wishes for its behavior. For good reason: Indeed our rational mind is as split off from the "reptilian brain" inside us within which these imprints circulate and from which they arise as are we from the consciousness of a gila monster.

What We Call "Reason" Is Largely Just Rationalization

This impotence of intellectual understanding in the face of these patterns of self-destruction occurs because these schemas are rooted in memories existing in an emotional and entirely dissociated part of the brain, which is hardly touched by neocortical admonishing of any kind. As deMause correctly points out,

[The fetus's] early experiences have been found to be recorded in a separate early neural network — a dissociated emotional memory system centering in the amygdala, quite distinct from the declarative memory system centering in the hippocampus that is established in later childhood.[2]

Disclaiming these cycles, which inevitably pass through darkness, and reliance on "will-power" to change one's patterns, which includes self-sabotage, has been exposed in its impotence in modern times. We see as evidence the growing acknowledgment of the ineffectiveness and, indeed, counter-effectiveness of psychoanalysis.[3]

Railing Against the Darkness

So the question begging to be asked is "What do we do about it?" What do we do about these pernicious cycles?

And when these elements erupt in society in harmless, possibly healing ways, how do we view them? Do we, as Mayr and Boelderl do in their article, "The Pacifier Craze: Collective Regression in Europe," decry the regression ... as if by disclaiming it we could somehow keep the cycle from happening?[4]

Mayr and Boelderl write, for example, that the situation of collective regression in Europe "strikes us as being high-explosive [sic] and bitter enough."[5]

In another place they exclaim, *"What is horrible* about this insight [about the increasing collective regression in Europe] is the additional observation that regression is becoming still more radical."[6]

This response of railing against the "Darkness" is a Freudian response. Yet it is not even a neo-Freudian one, since regression in the service of the ego — which began to be seen as ever more important by neo-Freudians — is not acknowledged, let alone considered.

Social Progress Requires Regression

That regression in the service of the ego is not considered is confirmed by Mayr and Boelderl in their statement that "Regression by definition is a process of repression and a defense mechanism."[7]

These are surprising words, in light of the concept of regression in the service of the ego and awareness of the clinically based evolution of psychotherapeutic theory since Freud's original postulations, nearly a century ago.

They are even more awry if one considers the universal, cross-cultural, implementation by societies of rebirthing rituals to handle the same kinds of forces we are confronted with. The anthropological literature is rife with these accounts.

Further, Grof has meticulously shown that regularly going into altered states of consciousness where one confronts this material is a prime function of cultures, and it occurs nearly universally although it is woefully lacking in Western culture for the most part.

Moreover, these words by Mayr and Boelderl indicate a conflict with or ignorance of the fact that deMause's theory of evolution of historical change requires regression on the part of parents, while parenting their children, as the primary "engine" of sociopsychological progress.

For deMause writes,

The ultimate source of all historical change is psychogenesis, the lawful change in childrearing modes occurring through generational pressure.... Psychogenesis depends upon the ability of parents and surrogates to regress to the psychic age of their children and work through the anxieties of that age better the second time than in their own childhood." (op. cit., 1982, p. 135, emphasis mine.)

But this mistake by these two social scientists would not be all that important if it was not the perfect example of the kind of uninformed *attitude* we have, generally speaking, in Western societies about these forces. This attitude is reinforced by a Judeo-Christian tradition of specialness and scapegoating in the West. It is a pervasive *feeling* about these things; specifically it, itself, is the actual defense. While this is a widespread reaction to our inner realities it is far from science, and even further from the truth or reality about these things.

"Stop It!" … Yeah, That's Gonna Work

At any rate, if we adopt this Western, Judeo-Christian, Freudian tactic of decrying the darkness, we are as effective in derailing the cycle of violence and war as Freudians are in what amounts to admonishing their clients to "stop it!" when it comes to *their* neurotic self-sabotaging.

For people cannot will themselves to merely stop their cycles of neurotic self-sabotage and self-destruction, which are the individual manifestations/ acting out of their birth traumas. As mentioned these directors of action operate out of a different part of the psyche, and brain, than one's conscious willing part. They are simply not accessible, so hardly amenable, to rational or willful input. And changing one's thoughts to affect them is about as helpful as rearranging the furniture on the deck of the Titanic to keep *it* from sinking.

Regression in the Service of the Ego

With the exposure of the ineffectiveness of the Freudian tactic of intellectual understanding has come the Freudian movement's disintegration into schools advocating various other strategies for change.

These schools/strategies include the psychiatric — the use of drugs; the neo-Freudians who acknowledge and use regression in the service of the ego and abreaction; the humanistic-existential approaches, stressing the "experiential"; and the Jungians and neo-Jungians, who would seek the resolution of these cycles in their inner archetypal acting out, resulting in an eventual rootedness of the ego in a higher Self (a spiritual center) beyond or transcending the cycles.[8]

Other approaches include the bulk of the spiritual, new-age, or transpersonal means that are flourishing these days. These alternative paths basically differ from all others in their belief that one can simply bypass these perinatal pulls and pushes and go directly to the Light or the Self by dismissing the birth cycles, or the Darkness or Shadow, through affirming the Light, meditating the Darkness out or the Light in, changing one's thoughts, creating one's reality, and various combinations of these.

Finally, these newer schools and strategies for healing include those of what might be called experiential psychotherapy, which includes primal therapy, holotropic breathwork, some forms of (experiential) meditation (Vipassana meditation, for example), Reichian and bioenergetic approaches, some forms of hypnotherapy — experiential ones — ones that involve reliving traumas — and virtually all the techniques, treatments, and correctives that are espoused in the field of pre- and perinatal psychology.

The point is that from a good number of these other-than-Freudian perspectives — and all of those that acknowledge the importance of regression in the service of the ego — and from the perspective of the entire field of experiential psychotherapy, the answer to the cycles of violence, war, and death-rebirth is to stop the acting out, not by simply intellectually decrying it — as if one can actually talk oneself out of one's inner fears and one's Darkness/Shadow — but by reliving those cycles of violence at their origins ... their *primal* roots. In the case of perinatal forces, those forces from "the dark side," this is accomplished by reliving the violence of birth, a perinatal trauma that is thoroughly and masterfully delineated by Grof and deMause.[9]

Auspicious Collective Regressions

But from this perspective of experiential psychotherapy — one completely congruent with and grateful of deMause's contributions in psychohistory as well — regression, in Europe, or elsewhere, is not seen as something to decry, disclaim, be horrified of, or be seen as dangerous but is seen as an opportunity. Regression is certainly not seen as a form of defense but as the opposite of that. *Regression is part of a process of diminishing one's defenses against one's internal reality of pain and trauma.*

Thus, examples of blatant collective regression as in Europe — more so to the extent they are relived, released, and integrated — are entirely auspicious for the eventual elimination of war as a collective device of acting out — defending against — the painful feelings coming from one's personal history which one carries around, all unknowingly, and which pervade, in one way or another, in forms subtle and not so subtle, every moment of one's consciousness in the present.

From this experiential psychotherapeutic perspective, we have a different feeling about developments like those that Mayr and Boelderl describe as collective regression in Europe and Lawson describes as occurring at rock concerts.[10]

From a more enlightened viewpoint these cultural phenomena should have us, if not dancing in the streets, at least hopeful of a gradual decrease in the use of war and violence. Why? It is because the youth who display this "regression" so blatantly were brought up by a more "advanced" form of child-rearing than that of previous generations, so they have fewer defenses, fewer layers of obfuscation covering up their unconscious psychodynamics. Consequently the regression is seen more clearly in their behavior.[11]

Unflinching Belief Related to Total Dissociation

Why is this important? DeMause points out that people do go to war, and that prior to it their perinatal dynamics come to the fore, as evidenced by perinatal-laden words and images in the media and in leaders' speeches used to describe the situation and its dynamics. Thus, our leaders take us into war, they act out their perinatal dynamics … and we in following them act out ours … in such gruesomely overt ways because these dynamics are so hidden, repressed, and overlaid with defenses that the conscious mind has absolutely no access to, and hence insight into, them as being part of one's unconscious dynamics.

Consequently the conscious mind is completely able to convince itself that those dynamics are actual, real, and doubtless parts of the situation and therefore require an actual, real, and extreme response. The amount of resolve required to act out war can only be wrought of an unflinching belief in the rightness, the absolute correctness of one's perspective of the situation and therefore of that extreme course of response. And that can only be brought about by a total dissociation from one's perinatal traumas, and a complete and utter projection of it on the outside — the enemy, to be specific.

Blatant "Sickness" Related to Being Real

The contrary is also true: When there does not exist that total and complete dissociation of the perinatal trauma — when it is, as in Europe and rock concerts currently, closer to the surface, less defended against, less repressed and, hence, more blatant — it is more accessible to consciousness and less likely to be acted out in the extreme as in war. Instead it is more likely to be acted out in less extreme forms, such as jumping into mosh pits, carrying pacifiers, listening to baby tunes about the, very real, difficulties of being a baby, and so on.

Finally, it is more likely to be actually allowed to emerge in consciousness and be relived, and thereby "healed" … and gone beyond, to be replaced by something more benign and more socially constructive, and thus to be removed forever as a motivation to war or violence. This is the auspicious view of the developments described by Mayr and Boelderl.[12]

Janov was the first to point out that a permanent resolution of underlying trauma initially entailed an aggravation of symptoms and symbolic acting out. That is to say, the underlying dynamics become more blatant and apparent in behavior.[13]

Janov was also the first to note that the acting-out and overt neurotic was closer to being "real," and therefore really sane, than his or her highly functioning and "normal," but repressed, rigidly defended, and unfeeling neighbor.[14]

Evolution of Parenting — We've Been Getting Saner

Finally, the correctness of the view that being "crazy" in an insane world might be more sane has been borne out in recent history. DeMause describes an evolution of parenting from ancient times to the present which involved ever decreasing psychosis and violence and increasing caring and consciousness of the needs of children. He connects this decrease in violent child caring to ever decreasing violence and psychotic acting out in societies.

DeMause labels the most common modern parenting mode the *socializing* mode. Short of the quite recent *helping mode* — which only really rose to prominence in the last three decades — the socializing mode is the most advanced and most humane.

Lest there be any confusion, I wish to point out that my own theoretical understanding differs from deMause's in one important respect. While I agree with his evolution of child-rearing over the course of civilization and within recorded time, I believe he is wrong about prehistory and what primal peoples were like and the kind of child-caring they engaged in. He depicts prehistoric societies as psychotically oblivious of the needs of children, engaging in, first, infanticidal; then, second, abandoning; then, third, ambivalent modes of child-rearing. Whereas it seems to me the overwhelming evidence and increasing numbers of anthropologists point to a natural "organic" child-caring being employed in the mists of the past quite a bit more "advanced" than even many modes employed today.

I believe the change from the loving parenting we see in many primal peoples and in Nature among many of our planetmates to the infanticidal, abandoning, and ambivalent modes he has described for early historic cultures is a product of that ever increasing control of Nature that went into full gear with the agrarian revolution, some ten to twenty-five thousand years ago. So, I am saying that brutal parenting was a consequence of "civilization" and was at its worst at the beginnings of recorded time.

But I agree we have been gradually evolving to better modes of child-caring over the history of civilization to the most sane and psychologically beneficial modes employed in recent decades, which, you might want to note, are very much like the modes of the earliest humans. I describe why and how we lost our connection with Nature and loving ways of parenting — how we left "Eden" — in my book and blog *The Great Reveal*.

The Cycles of Time

I believe my understanding shows once again how much of what modern folks thought of "development" — including it being linear and increasing from "darkness" to "light" with ourselves always at the top (conveniently) — is wrong and merely part of an anthropocentric bias and an ethnocentric heritage. For more and more, as we lay down those blinders to reality, we notice the evidence of the cyclical nature of everything — from our lives (ashes to ashes) to the physical Universe's expansion and contraction, to the vibrations at the subatomic level, the waves in the sea, the turning of the Earth and the revolutions of the solar systems, and I contend now also, the so-called "history" of our species on Earth. This is the thoroughly postmodern idea that human time is also cyclical, with over and again peoples returning to earlier halcyon times only to "fall" away from them.

The Worst of Times Quality of Current Events

This idea of time as cyclical not linear is in keeping with Eastern philosophies, as well as indigenous ones. Hindu thinking currently has us at the depths of the Kali Yuga, the worst part of the cycle right now, with matters to be reversed very soon and the best of times just ahead. And, as I have been describing in my books *Falls from Grace* and *Primal Renaissance* and will be directly pointing out in my upcoming book, *Primal Return*, we are currently seeing a most necessary return to a more harmonious way of being and a more natural self. And with it, requiring it, to some extent preceding it, we are evolving to the most advanced mode of loving parenting.

The "Best of Times" Nature of Our Parenting

Psychohistorian Glenn Davis, following deMause, analyzed the most advanced form of child-caring short of the most recent helping mode — the psychogenic parenting mode deMause termed *socializing* — and found that it comprised four submodes. In order, beginning in the mid-nineteenth century to the mid-twentieth century and each one a more "evolved" and humane one than the previous one, they are the submodes of psychic control, aggressive training, vigorous guidance, and delegated release.[15]

Oh, Be-HAVE. WWII Generation … Received Aggressive-Training and Vigorous-Guidance Parenting

Davis concluded that in America the Vietnam War was perpetrated by individuals belonging almost entirely to the *aggressive-training* and *vigorous-guidance* psychoclasses.[16]

Questioning Authority and Oneself Is Good. Boomers ... Received Delegated Release Parenting

Yet the Vietnam War was brought to an end largely as a result of the efforts of an antiwar movement whose largest component was a Sixties youth brought up under a more advanced *delegated-release* child-caring mode.[17]

The delegated release mode, which resulted in the phenomenon of Sixties youth and the counterculture, is the most "advanced" mode short of the helping mode.

"Let's Collaborate" — Millennials. Received the Most Advanced Parenting — Helping ... "We Just Want You to Be Happy."

The *helping* mode is the child-caring mode employed widely by the Sixties generation for their children, the Millennial Generation, also known as Generation Y. So, a helping mode of parenting was enjoyed by the children of a delegated-release psychoclass, the Boomers. Sixties youth are seen, psychologically, to have the most the most "advanced" ego structures short of their children taught within a helping mode.[18]

Walking In Another's Moccasins

It is obvious that these Sixties youth did not have the same unflinching and unqualified belief in the absolute rightness of their country's position in Vietnam as did many of their parents. This is obviously the case in a psychoclass of youth chanting a generational mantra, "Question authority!" and whose more extreme members would at times even go over to the perspective of seeing the war from the eyes of the "enemy," the Other.

As I mentioned earlier, among the Sixties Generation we saw Jane Fonda's journey to Hanoi, the waving of North Vietnamese flags by protesters, and the carrying of little red books on the sayings of Chairman Mao. These are obvious indicators that the generation as a whole was open to seeing the war from the North Vietnamese perspective: That is, as a conflict perpetrated by a foreign nation that was hypocritical in its espousal of democracy in that it prevented democratic elections that would have without doubt elected Ho Chi Minh and instead it installed a puppet-ruler in the South, making Vietnam a virtual colony of the United States. From this perspective, the Vietnam War was for the Vietnamese as much a war for independence as the American Revolution was for the U.S.

This is just an example of how there are two sides to every issue and how an attempt at empathy or "walking in The Other's moccasins" — made possible by a closeness to a perinatal unconscious that is also an opposite perspective than that of the conscious mind — can lead, at the minimum, to the reluctance necessary to prevent engaging in at least the most blatant and horrific forms of violence ... against others, but consider also, against Nature.

The Perinatal Generation

At any rate, is there evidence that this undermining of the self-righteous position necessary for the instigation and carrying out of war and ecocide — this ability to see at least somewhat from The Other's perspective and not just one's own — is in truth correlated with a closeness to perinatal dynamics, a closeness to the unconscious for that generation of youth, those of the Sixties? The answer: Absolutely yes!

As mentioned in a previous part, sociologist Kenneth Keniston did psychological studies of members of the Sixties Generation.

He was inspired to do so through his noticing that he was seeing something really unusual and radically different in these youth than what he had ever seen. This led to his fascination with discovering what made them so different. And he documented his findings in two books — *The Uncommitted: Alienated Youth in American Society* and *Young Radicals: Notes on Committed Youth*. Roughly speaking he chose to study the unconscious dynamics of both the "alienated-hippie" and the "activist" sectors, respectively, of that generation.[19]

Blushing Troll-Handlers

At the risk of repeating myself, I wish to remind the reader that a reading of his books — keeping in mind that Keniston knew nothing of perinatal dynamics at that time, and few people did, for that matter — reveals a degree of perinatal imagery, fantasy, and acting out — especially among "the uncommitted" — enough to make a troll-handling, pacifier-wearing, mosh-pit jumping youth of today to blush![20]

Self-Analysis and Psychological-Mindedness

Because of this peculiar perinatal access, I don't believe it is any coincidence that Keniston also found an unusual amount of inner reflection — questioning oneself — alongside the more well-known questioning authority. This he labeled "overexamined life" for the alienated sector and "psychological mindedness" for the activists.

Better Emotionally Disturbed Than "Healthily" Engaging in War

So, being close to one's perinatal imprints, being less defended against one's inner unconscious painful memories, leads to one being able to question not just oneself — and therefore to be a catalyst to personal growth and a quest for truth — but also the actions of one's society. It is a counterbalance to our tendency to act out in violence to others as in war and to Nature as in ecocide. It means people will suffer more inner turmoil and pain, will feel more psychologically "disturbed," and will be less likely to take it out on others, will be less likely to make others or the environment "pay" for what happened to them.

Let us contrast that with its opposite. DeMause writes,

Hitler's projection of his fears ... into Jews and foreigners helped him avoid a psychotic breakdown and enabled him to function during his later life, as long as others shared his delusion of poisonous enemies.

Therefore acting out collectively, as in war, can prevent a psychotic breakdown in certain individuals.

Better Psychotic Than Waging War

But when the consequences of acting out one's birth trauma, collectively, is millions of people — including oneself — dead, not to mention the uncountably large loss of material and personal resources, it is clear that by comparison a psychotic breakdown is a more benign alternative for either the individual or the society in which that or those individuals act.

Similarly, not providing the outlet of war as a collective birth ritual ... oftentimes, for the soldier involved, euphemistically called a "rite of passage" ... would allow the genuine neurotic breakdowns, the collapse of people's defenses, and their opening up to their underlying perinatal dynamics. Thus accessed, they can be healed, or in the least they would prevent the kind of unflinching belief or self-righteousness required for war and violence.

Some folks might even be motivationally paralyzed — receiving information from the unconscious that contradicts and undermines the stance and beliefs of their conscious ego. But when that egoistic stance is slanted, commonly, towards war, violence, selfishness and greed and corresponding environmental apathy, then better one would be indecisive, overwhelmed, and doing nothing.

The Price of Emotional Pain Is Minuscule Compared to That of War

Yet it is true that this neurotic breakdown, of at least a small amount, on the scale of society would result in the kind of collective regressions that Mayr and Boelderl, and Lawson describe. That is, the cause of peace, of the saving of human lives, requires that people pay the price of encountering their primal pain.

By all measures, this peace price is minuscule. It is even more worth it when you take into account the fact that many people, after initially "breaking down" for lack of a collective ... and highly destructive ... act-out like war/aggression, will actually succeed in reconstructing a self that is more in line with reality, through the dynamics and means categorized under the term *regression in the service of the ego, described above.* Regardless of professional help ... which would be nice but is not always available or practical ... some people just find a way.

CHAPTER 10

WHERE THERE IS HOPE, CULTURAL REBIRTHING

Societal Self-Analysis

Culture War Replaced Cold War

We see the workings of these opposing tendencies to look away from problems or to embrace them by examining the reactions in America to the collapse of the Soviet Union. The disappearance of this huge object for distraction from inner unhappiness, about which one could rationalize the use of defensiveness and scapegoating, led to continued turning away through the emergence, in America, of a search for other societal scapegoats and therefore the "Republican revolution." Culture War replaced the Cold War as the way one could be comfortably ignorant of one's insides and self-assuredly distracted, self-righteously engaged.

This removal of a collective punching bag or scapegoat also resulted in a healthy turning toward the darkness within and a collective self-analysis in America. This reaction has brought to the fore many of our social and political shortcomings.

Talk Show Soul-Searching

For evidence of this latter response we notice beginning in the Nineties the rise of the talk show; the rituals of nationwide self-examination over issues of sexual harassment, spouse abuse, and race relations played out in the Anita Hill — Clarence Thomas hearings and the O. J. Simpson trial; the hashing out of controversial and formerly hidden personal issues around sex, lies, and marital fidelity, played out in the Clinton-Lewinsky Scandal; the reevaluation of matters of faith precipitated by priestly sexual abuse; and many other such national psychodramas staged on cable news networks and the magazine-style, documentary-type TV shows like *Frontline, Nightline* and the like.

We also witnessed the rise of reality shows as part of this societal pull to see beneath the covers of what is thought to be real. Now, progressives and intellectuals have lots of fun vamping about how superior they themselves are to such interests, as exemplified in reality shows. This can only be the position of elitists out of touch with the ways ordinary folks live their lives.

Sitcom Socialization

To make my point, let me back up a bit. The swagger that the Left, and intellectuals in general, display around reality shows is the same superiority they have expressed for decades concerning sitcoms. First, let me say that I consider most sitcoms and reality shows to be rather boring and a bit inane with their laugh and soundtrack framing. Yet, when I was a child, growing up in a medium-sized city in the coal country of Pennsylvania and coming from a very traditional family, it was only through such sitcoms that I had a chance to find out what a different style of family and parenting would be. Today, I would laugh at a *Father Knows Best*. But it was a step up and into socialization from the "Father Knows

Little" or "Father Not Around" of many in my social stratum when I was a kid. This exposure allowed me, and many of my generation, to seek for more in our life and for better interpersonal family relationships ... and eventually better parenting.

This presentation of better alternatives — middle-class, liberal, "hollywood" ones — to everyone in America has a lot to do with the fact that the Sixties were so explosive. It was the first decade after the introduction of a national culture through the medium of television. Much has been made of the fact that newscasts brought information into living rooms for the first time in that era — which is the thing that intellectual elitists will focus on, blinded by their quaint beliefs that humans are rational actors. It takes an experiential psychologist and social scientist like myself to notice that most folks act out of ideas and attitudes that are rooted in experiences and information that are hardly rational. So, the modeling of a more "advanced" way of family life — not perfect but for many better than the traditional ways they had known, which included things like spanking and attitudes like "children are better seen not heard" and "spare the rod, spoil the child" — through the TVs and cinemas of America was vastly more influential in changing society than newscasts, whose information could just as easily have been shared through the print media. The sitcoms brought liberal middle-class values to everyone in America who owned a tv set; and this was a huge step forward at the time.

A Modern "Priesthood"

This is where righties have it right when targeting "hollywood" for many of the changes in our culture over the last half century ... though they see that as a negative influence. But intellectuals and lefties blow an opportunity and lose support among ordinary folks through an unconscious haughtiness and a cultural snobbery they are blind to but display in their turning up their noses at popular culture. Luckily, as an anthropological social scientist, I can study popular culture and get away with it, though not without some snide commentary coming my way from progressive and professional circles. They simply will never understand an intellectual who can speak to working folks because he is one of them. They simply do not get my attempts to package the crucial understandings of modern science and social sciences, on which the existence of our very world depends, in words that are not primarily directed to and meant to appease the gods of academia. They consider themselves important within their tiny professional circles, thinking they are changing the world when no one even knows what they are doing beyond that constrained perimeter.

Keeping the People Down

Indeed the attitude of academics and progressives about popular culture, especially talk and reality show TV programming and although they would be appalled to ever think it, is no different from the attitudes of the Catholic Church and the clergy about matters of faith during medieval times. There, too, we had an elite wanting to "keep out the unwashed." There, too, we had a distinction between people in the know and the rabble, with the anointed ones requiring ordinary folks to go through them for matters of truth and faith. We had then also this sharp distinction between the "high culture" of the Church and aristocracy — exemplified in the chamber music of the time — and the "low culture" of the masses — exemplified by the folk music of the troubadours of that day.

Nowadays this poo-pooing of TV culture by intellectuals is the same kind of attempt to funnel reality to the masses through the filters of a new "priesthood." The cultural purists and intellectual elites would prefer that for truth you go through them in academia, where you have to pay a toll of course, just as the priests of the Middle Ages required you to pass their way on the road to the divine.

Therapy for the Masses

At any rate throwing off the snootiness of intellectualism, I contend, allows us to notice that sitcoms, reality shows, and talk shows serve functions in society that are, overall, beneficial in advancing our culture and catalyzing increased growth. They may not reflect, yet, where intellectuals and progressives think we should be, but for many they show something beyond where they are.

We should know that they are overall helpful in our cause from the fact that conservatives want to attack hollywood and limit freedom of expression on any airwave. The fact that many reactionaries want to keep their children out of schools, home-schooled, and away from TV sets should be telling progressives something about the value of popular culture.

Rebirth Denied

My point is that the rise in reality and talk shows are coincident with a need for a kind of societal "therapy" that came about when we took back our projections from the Soviets and were forced to look at ourselves. I am saying this was a healthy way of doing it, and this was helping us, though it was tumultuous and difficult, in the Nineties. It is unfortunate, but it suited the forces of war and fascism, for the 1% to bring forth in the millennium the bugaboo of terrorism ... perfectly bringing about another endless feud with another concocted enemy to project our own darknesses onto so we can escape from having to notice them ourselves and bring about actual personal growth and cultural advance ... let alone the cultural rebirth that has been trying to happen for decades.

American Rehab

Reality shows are like watching group therapy happening. It is not surprising that there was even one reality program that was about therapy — Celebrity Rehab. Reality shows also expose ordinary folks to what amounts to crude but informative sociological experiments. If academics could see beyond their pretensions they would applaud this sort of, however haphazard and imprecise, understanding of group processes and individual psychology arising in the masses.

If there weren't reality shows, folks would have a harder time knowing appropriate ways for men and women to act with each other. The gains of feminism would not have spread so widely or as fast if they were not being modeled and reinforced repeatedly on talk and reality shows. They demonstrate parenting and social skills — "politically correct" ones, in the good sense — to folks who would otherwise not know any better than to behave crudely and abusively. They bring the world, geography, travel, and history to the masses.

Intellectuals quibble about the quality of that, which comes across as quite childish, for it arises as if out of a jealousy of others getting the attention they want and out of a fear of competition for informational matters around science, culture, and humanities. It strikes me as more than ironic that those on the Left who would wish people to wake up from their zombie slumber would want to push programs of literature or drama where truths are filtered through the consciousness, and unconscious, of the artist, while wishing to deprive folks of a direct look — however contrived, it is actual reality and not scripted — at the world around them and people's actual unplanned behavior and spontaneous reactions to unusual events.

Seeing people's behavior in some of these shows does often remind me of the dynamics I have seen in therapy groups, and some of the personal changes in the participants mirror some of the evolutions I have seen in folks undergoing deep experiential psychotherapy. The audience participation part often sounds like group therapy or an intervention. I have been struck by how some of the group processes in the show remind me of family day in rehab, with folks reflecting back what they see in each other and how others' behavior has affected them. These are all things that conservatives cringe at … actually *hate*. Yet liberals, except for notable exceptions like Jerry Springer, are not seeing the opening they have here. Lefties are fighting rather than using these forces, which are in the direction of personal growth and, cumulatively, much needed societal change.

As a psychologist and simply someone who loves people, I am fascinated by some of the things I see in these shows. They can be heart-wrenchingly real at times. So it occurs to me that folks who disparage these shows, comparing them with literature and dramatic productions, is another thing where some are wanting to have their reality filtered, managed, and packaged for them, lest it be too "disruptive" to their prejudices of things.

The Price of Peace Is Inner Sight

The upshot of all this is to say that just as a lack of a Cold War caused both collective acting out — another war, a Culture War — and collective inner searching via television talk shows, documentaries, and such. So also the prevention of "hot" wars on an international, not just intercultural, scale and the cause of peace in general require such inner soul-searching and such confrontation with one's darker sides. And if we must, it is better to endure the psychotic acting out of a culture war — with its battles played out on the airwaves — than an actual war.

For is there any doubt that either of these or any combinations of these alternatives, however uncomfortable and even violent … on a smaller scale … at times, is a small price to pay compared to the price of outright war and violence which, by any measurement, is a cost horrifyingly huge and unacceptable?

America Currently Refusing to Pay Such Price

The converse of this is also true: When the dramas wanting to be discussed are suppressed in the mainstream media, it is as stifling of the growth of a nation as an individual's growth. Unfortunately we have seen this as well recently. There have been massive worldwide and nationwide Occupy Wall Street demonstrations, massive Wisconsin union outpourings, and events in Japan and about Fukushima that the American people really want to and need to know and discuss, but they are being blacklisted from being broadcasted on. There has been a change in government in Iceland, with banksters being jailed, that Americans are not hearing about; there have been demonstrations in Japan about their insane response to their tragedy, which Americans are not being told about; there have been massive demonstrations in Israel against the colonial policies of their own government that curiously do not make it into the offerings of news programs. These are things that in the Nineties would have fed the talk on TV and stimulated the necessary societal hashing out for there to be a chance of going beyond them.

What Is the Cost of Denial? Of Complacency?

It is hard to know, though, what happens when the natural urges of a nation to grow and change are thwarted. While I discussed this abortion of cultural renewal and the abomination that results from it at length in Chapter Seven of a companion book to this one, *Culture War, Class War*, under the title "Cultural Rebirth, Aborted," the question remains what happens when this societal "rebirthing" is more urgent than ever. What happens when — for the sake of the survival of the human race and of the planet — it is necessary that this growth happen and instead it is continuously derailed and snuffed out of the light of collective consciousness?

Internet Revolution Is Another Reformation

Luckily all this is changing as the internet and social networking have upended the academic elitists, swarming around and over their petty barriers of intellectual privilege. The blogsters and "rabble" of the net have taken over the cultural dialogue of the time as assuredly as Martin Luther and the Reformation changed religion forever and helped to bring to an end the cultural stagnation of the Middle Ages and to ignite an Age of Reason and of Enlightenment.

"Know Thyself" ~ "Narcissistic"?

Self-Discovery, Soul-Searching, Psychological-Mindedness, Self-Analysis — Sixties Generation

So, we have taken a look at the need for societies to "do therapy" on themselves, to hash out and process, however messy that might seem to be, the perinatal projections from the unconscious, as they manifest in the tribulations of the times — both profound and mundane. It must be kept in mind that it is the products of nearly the most "advanced" mode of child-caring — the delegated-release subclass of the socializing psychoclass — who have proved most willing to pay such prices for peace, as for example, in increased soul-searching. In fact they would be later stigmatized for just this quality of introspection, this supposed fault of looking into themselves, through the derogatory appellation, *narcissistic.*

Indeed, Keniston foresaw this when he studied the Sixties generation as college students. Observing the amount of inner exploration they engaged in during their quests for self-discovery, he would describe this attribute in a biased way as "the overexamined life," and more fairly, for the activist youth, as a "psychological-mindedness" and "self-analysis."[1]

"Let It All Out? No, Leave Some of It In!" — Pat Buchanan, Fifties Generation

No doubt those who criticized these youth in the past are some of the same ones or their surrogates who, now older, are wrongly castigating the self-analyzing characteristics of contemporary society as the Sixties generation is now in its "triumphant" phase — the time when as adults a psychoclass takes over the reins of society and most strongly influences it. I have already taken note of the tendencies of the right to rile against the collective processing that is happening in their attacks on popular culture and in particular what they call "hollywood." They express their desire that "such matters" not come to public light, for they deem them "offensive" or an affront to their (oh so delicate) sensibilities. They sense a threat to the precious untruths that prop up their self-destructive way of life, woven through as it is with war, fascism, planetary and planetmate annihilation, and the other horrors mushrooming about them in the postmodern era.[2]

These highly defended and fear-minded conservatives, prone to projection, are incapable of appreciating the integrity of an inner-thinking generation like the Boomers are. These outer-minded authoritarians would not get, would outright hate those who "questioned authority" in the Sixties.

These defended entrenched egos would be secretly jealous of and overtly aggressive to a generational emergence that since the Sixties has been psychologically, emotionally, and spiritually working on themselves to be free of inner tyranny. As one of their exemplars, Pat Buchanan, long ago phrased it, "Let it all out? No, leave some of it in!"

Let the Buck Stop Here!

Nonetheless this cadre of kindred Sixties spirits would in their actions declare for the first time in history as a generation, "Let the buck stop here!" And they would seek to turn themselves, and by extension their children and society-at-large, into a more loving, wise, and less acting-out humanity ... most importantly, one willing to cooperate rather than war with Nature, or other nations.

If Not Us, Who? If Not Now, When?

What virtually all the folks outside "my generation" never get is the unimpeachable vision we had of the complete and utter wrongness of the path and tendencies of modern times and the abyss toward which civilization was heading. We were proven right, of course, as especially in the last decade we have seen the disintegration wrought of those tendencies on all fronts — political, environmental, personal. The Sixties generation saw modern civilization as being unreformable and needing complete remaking, so that everything we did was an attempt to create reality and culture from scratch, sans tradition.

We had seen normal ways of doing things to be impotent and often dangerous and most importantly leading to apocalyptic endings in our near future. This understanding is what was responsible for all the "non-normal" behaviors my generation displayed — communes, confrontations, clothes, relationships, organics, alternative ways of everything ... an entire counterculture. We have been laughed at for essentially being ahead of the curve on the messages of modern events. We have been called crazy for our inconvenient prophecies, virtually all of which are now coming to pass.

While I and my cohorts, to use just one example, spoke out on the dangers of nuclear energy and in particular the insanity of building plants on fault lines, the professional pundits scoffed and boasted they lived near nuclear plants. This was thirty years and more before the world ever heard the word, *Fukushima*. The examples like this are endless. We saw all these unworkable endings and asked ourselves, "What would be a *real* way of doing that?" "What would be a workable, sustainable way?" "What would be a sane and happy life, ethic, and lifestyle." "What would be a loving, peaceful mode of being?"

While we sought to redo culture from scratch, building it on perennial and unimpeachable principles, the threatened elders and the jealous youngers, who would soon enough come behind, poked fun from within the confines of their assured and comfortable wrongness. They called us narcissistic for thinking we could look at ourselves and the world and dare to think we could change it from ancient ways. They thought we were making ourselves important that way, putting on airs, even. Actually we were shouldering responsibility we did not want — yearning for a simpler, less serious time — but which we accepted for the sake of all those who would come after, knowing their very existence depended on our actions. We took faith in the touchstone of love itself — the only thing that did not crumble under examination — and sought to bend all emerging along its outlines.

So our seeming impertinence was born of an inconvenient prompting, an unwanted vision now proving prophetic. It was hardly selfish, as many of the best of my generation paid the ultimate price and are no longer with us or they are imprisoned. It was hardly narcissistic as it was done out of love ... for each other, for the peoples of all the world and of all the religions, for our children, for the planetmates and for the Nature of which we learned we were a part, and for the generations unborn.

What others will never get is that our "overexamined life," our "psychological-mindedness," our perinatal propensities, and our soul-searching and self-analysis were not about being narcissistic. It was about needing to start everything anew as a rational response to the horrors we saw about us in our culture and in the world ... horrors which we were correct in trying to address at the time. For their existence today, because of our inability to be completely successful in remedying them, are bringing about all the political, economic, and environmental armageddons I have been discussing in this, and its related, books. And we knew, and still know, that only some change huge and radical will help us, and for that we need to find and stand upon the deepest and firmest of ground within us. That is what we have been looking for, are still looking for ... only now we have lots of company.

A Drive to Healing

We cannot expect that everyone will heal their birth traumas when they arise into consciousness during periods of peace. However, we can expect — especially now that there is understanding of these dynamics and there are techniques and modalities available for healing them — that some people will!

Furthermore, even the more ritualistic and superficial yet blatant regressions to infancy, birth, prenatal, or even prior to that — for example, as Mayr and Boelderl describe in Europe — are not the indication of a "death drive" or "death instinct" as these researchers claimed.[3]

These highly symbolic collective rituals are instead the manifestations of a drive to healing — a drive to regressing to early traumas and to reexperiencing the events that occurred then and thus recapturing an integrity of self that existed prior to the dissociation that happened as a result of those traumas. This drive to regression is no more a "death wish" than the mystical or spiritual quest is a "death wish," and for the same reasons, as Jung correctly admonished Freud a long time ago. And we can expect that more good than bad can come, eventually, from engaging in them.

What Did You Expect Peace to Look Like?

Better Hitler Had Jumped Into Mosh Pits

In conclusion, when we see blatant collective regressions, by the sorts of people mentioned, to these perinatal dynamics in undisguised, and relatively harmless, social rituals — as described by Mayr and Boelderl, and Lawson — we can expect that, because of their closeness to their unconscious pain, they are likely — even if only a little more likely because of their more advanced mode of child-caring — to have insight into these dynamics and to resist acting them out in a more extreme form, like war, global pollution, and overpopulation.

To put it another way, I would have preferred that Hitler had acted out his craziness by jumping into mosh pits, humming baby tunes, wearing a pacifier ... or even engaging in sexual orgies ... than the way he did.

So these current signs of blatant regression by youth and others in Europe or the US, or in fact anywhere in the world as in rock concerts, are not signs of an impending war. What did you expect peace to look like? You might call it messy, but it is the scenery of human healing, we should expect to be seeing, on the pathway to an Earth rebirth.

What Might We Expect?

Millennial Promise

What might we expect from the future? Well if ecological/environmental consciousness and refusal to use projection onto others is accepted as evidence of perinatal access, as I have been asserting, then the current generation of youth and young adults — the Baby-Boomer Echo Generation, also called the Millennial Generation, whose two main concerns, as I have mentioned, have been polled as being the environment and racism — may also be expected to be more open to their perinatal trauma, and hence more likely to resolve it and further the gains of their parents against war and global apocalypse.

"A Hard Rain's Gonna Fall"

For, as Janov has pointed out, closer to one's Pain — one's unconscious — is closer to being real. And this closeness holds out the possibility both of healing ... and of self-destruction.

From the roads and TV screens of America the scenery can often appear bleak. Sure, heavy changes are coming down ... but what should we expect? "A hard rain's gonna fall," sang Bob Dylan. And that's what it takes to blossom the spring. Look hard enough, you just might see the seeds of Light amidst the darkness surrounding.

Evidence in Our Collective Dreaming

Next we will take a look at one of the projective systems of our society, specifically, our cinema, to see if it shows evidence of the change of consciousness that we have here been describing as necessary to derail the cycles of war and violence that have plagued our species for millennia uncountable and have led us to the brink of extinction.

Films are both the collective dreams of our society as well as the only truly widely shared method of collectively experiencing a nonordinary state of consciousness. Thus they are telling, in the messages they contain, as well as powerful in their impact on the audience, who in this mild nonordinary state of consciousness are more open to suggestion and to receiving mental impressions and information.

We will look to examples from films of the last few decades for indications that our collective consciousness is actually changing and that there are grounds for hoping that we will be able to stave off apocalypse ... creating instead the quantum leap to an Earth rebirth.

CHAPTER 11

CONTROL VERSUS SURRENDER … HEAVEN LEADS THROUGH HELL

Is there any evidence that the changes that need to happen for us to stave off apocalypse and save our world are actually occurring?

The "Royal Road" to Our Collective Mind

I have mentioned there are studies of the psychology of generations, beginning with the Baby-Boomers or Sixties Generation, that show both an increased access to the perinatal as well as a tendency to act out perinatal influences in less harmful … though more blatant … ways than generations prior. We have seen that this tendency goes hand in hand with actual engagement in activities to counter the negative perinatal act-outs that exist in our environment, for example, campaigning against war, pollution, racism, violence, and so on.

But in "Chapter Three: The Perinatal Media," I introduced the common anthropological tenet that the projective systems of a culture — that is, its art and artifacts — can be analyzed to get a glimpse into the worldview of a particular society. For our purposes, I pointed out how our movies are especially potent glimpses into our collective consciousness as well as our collective unconscious. You might say that our cinema is the "royal road" to our collective unconscious.

Movies As Collective Dreaming

Our flicks perform admirably well as collective dreams in that, unlike the other products of our collective consciousness such as other art and artifacts, they are multimedia stories, much like dreams are. But more than that, they are shared by more of the populace than any other art form. I am not including TV separately as an art form, since I put it in the same category as films, especially when many films are broadcast on TV and much else on TV also has the same character of being multimedia stories.

Finally, the strength of a particular element of the collective consciousness can be easily determined by the popularity of a particular movie that represents it or by that element's increasing inclusion in a number of films. For example, in "The Perinatal Media, " I discussed the emerging new elements of faces coming out of walls and forceful oral insertion.

Putting Our Society "on the Couch"

All together, these mean that, just as a psychotherapist might analyze a client's dreams to get an idea of his or her unconscious workings and contents, one can interpret mainstream movies to get an idea of the workings and contents of our society's "collective mind" — both conscious and unconscious.

This is no more complex than saying that when we see things in movies that people rush to see, they are drawn to it because those things are also in their own minds. And the more they flock — the greater the success of a movie — the more pervasive in a society are those themes, elements, and contents. Certain aspects — themes or elements in films — are said to really "resonate" with people and therefore people make the movies that contain them popular and successful.

When this is said, it only means that people are consciously or unconsciously drawn to things that exist within themselves. Conversely, no existence inside? No interest.

So in this and upcoming chapters I will use films as the dreaming out loud of our collective mind. Put less esoterically, I will be analyzing a few examples of mainstream movies for their content, and I will be assuming the content I find there exists as well in the society that has watched it … has *dreamt* it.

I will also be assuming that movies that are mainstream, by which I mean can be found readily for sale as DVDs on-line or in retail stores and have become part of the popular conversation are indicative of pervasive elements in our collective consciousness and unconscious. They can be looked at for the unacknowledged workings of our society as a whole.

I will not deal with the actual numbers of people who have attended particular movies. For I will assume out of the tens of thousands of movies that are produced each year — by small and large producers — those that have made it into the theaters of virtually all the communities of our society, and from there onto the DVD lists and the shelves of stores of all those communities, have by those facts alone demonstrated their resonance with the collective social mind. Otherwise, we would get into the maelstrom of analyzing critic's opinions of these movies; and with that, to modify a saying, opinions are like asses: everyone has a different one.

Something's Happening Here ... Again

One final point about the heuristic value of the analysis of films for the workings of the collective mind: Elements and themes in movies change over time. I have shown how new elements may be evidence of new elements of our collective unconscious minds coming into consciousness in detailing how the faces-in-the-wall element has developed. (See "Faces Coming Out of the Walls" in Chapter Three.)

But when old, familiar plots have different outcomes, this is important as well. When elements change or evolve over time, this speaks of something going on. This points to changes or evolutions in our collective consciousness. And when elements and themes and plots change or evolve rapidly, we can accurately say that the changes in consciousness are equally swift. (See, for example, "Fear and Freedom ... Only a Membrane Away" in Chapter Three.)

These are some of the tools we will be using in this and upcoming chapters as we take a look at a few examples of mainstream films and what they might be reflecting back to us about our own society's changes in consciousness. But first let me say something about what may turn out to be the most important of the thematic evolutions or changes in film elements that we have been seeing.

Information Avalanche and Pre- and Perinatal Themes

In the last half century we have been hearing a great deal about the need to expand consciousness to balance the negative effects of the extremes of technological advance. Fortunately this change of consciousness is to some extent inevitable — or at least greatly aided — by certain side effects of the technological explosion ... specifically in the area of telecommunications.

Ego-Eroding Information Deluge

As cultural boundaries are eroded by a multicultural information avalanche, people are forced to lower their inner defenses and ego boundaries. Confronted by such incoming information people will either take some of it in, learn, and thereby grow beyond their former selves or they will need to expend themselves in an all-out effort to shore them up.

A potent example of the first, currently, is the way people worldwide are opening to and learning from each other using social media via the internet; the revolutionary potential of this creation of an open global consciousness is already showing itself in uprising for democracies and economic justice virtually everywhere on Earth. A clear example of the second — where folks are putting everything into blocking out information and beating back the personal growth that would result — is in the backlashes to these liberal forces, which are also occurring throughout the world — as a Tea Party in the United States and as the fortification of authoritarian regimes from China to Syria and Turkey, from Iran to Israel.

We have seen that the first response — where folks allow the discomfort inherent in personal growth — is typical of a more advanced form of child-caring that is centered on the needs of the child. We know also that the latter reaction goes with child-caring centered on the needs of the care-givers, or parents ... and *not* the child. In this latter instance of parenting, it is understandably called child-*rearing* or *raising* a child as opposed to *child-caring*. We have noticed that the first response goes along with increased self-analysis and introspection and the latter one with acting out, aggression, and culture war.

Information Tsunami Pushes Consciousness Revolution

So, this tsunami of information in all areas, where previously we could smugly hold forth ego-satisfying views, pushes both toward an overthrow of those narrower perspectives and the establishment of broader, more encompassing ones as well as toward an ever increasing irrationality in fending off this information, *at any and all costs.*

I discussed at length in a previous section how this informational upswelling has led to a need to process it all in new social formats and the rituals of the talk and reality shows.

"Consciousness Raising" As "Shoveling It"

For the most part, this growth or expansion of consciousness, when it happens, is seen as a linear increase and correspondingly is labeled a "raising" of consciousness. This is true whether we are talking about societal or individual progress.

Ken Wilber's transpersonal theory is the most popular version of such a ladder-style path. In it the process of growth is analogous to that of climbing a mountain or shoveling compost into a pickup truck — one simply moves upward or piles it on.[1]

But there are those who think otherwise.

The Path to Heaven Leads Through Hell

Those in the know about the pervasive pre- and perinatal influence on personality and behavior, and especially those of us actively engaged in working through the effects of such early traumas, are fully aware, like Dante, that the path to heaven leads through hell. We have found that the path to the transpersonal light leads through the psychodynamic and perinatal darkness, that the path up and the path down are parts of the same path outward.[2]

A Dark and Hideous Shadow World

Our experience has been that the information avalanche and multicultural onslaught have eroded our personal boundaries to an influx, not only of transpersonal bliss-love-compassion, but equally — and very often, initially — to a dark and hideous shadow world, a backwards bizarro world, of pernicious and insidious disorganized feelings comprised of elements ancient, infantile, pathological, biological, scatological, and perinatal. These are some of the forms spiritual emergence can take, especially initially. And they are the ones most likely to be seen as spiritual emergencies.

Pre- and Perinatal Themes in Cinema

Therefore, it is interesting to see these views confirmed by the bubbling up of psychodynamic and perinatal themes in our collective consciousness as evidenced by current films, books, and music. I have mentioned the pre- and perinatal themes and symbolism in films and explained why, along with other elements of postmodern times, they are evidence of something significant occurring in the consciousness of our age — an emerging perinatal unconscious.

But there is another element evolving in current films which has to do with a changing or evolving collective attitude toward these perinatal elements. And along with a changing attitude, there is evidence pointing to an evolving collective response to it.

Control Versus Surrender, Death Versus Life

"Control Spiritualities" and Patriarchal Cultures

Specifically, a different kind of heroic response, which characterizes the perinatal arena, can be said to characterize the postmodern movies replete with perinatal symbolism. Most striking of all, this different kind of heroic response corresponds to a different kind of spirituality than what is commonly portrayed in this society, or at least has been the norm up until now.

For basically there are "control" spiritualities and "surrender" spiritualities, with rarely the twain meeting. "Control spiritualities" are adapted to patriarchal cultures and involve the use of the ego to "control" and be in charge of even the realms of the supernatural. This is so because an ultimate evil — a devil or Satan — is postulated, which is given equal weight along with God in determining one's ultimate fate. This type of spirituality is normally what is called *religion*.

"Surrender Spiritualities" and God as Being Good

But there is another brand of spirituality that is based on a belief in the ultimate goodness and rightness of All That Is. God's goodness being essentially the dominant force in the Universe, herein it is considered safe to "surrender" in one's relation to Reality, to expect that one will be guided correctly, in fact perfectly, in the act of letting go. Thus letting go is not to be feared — as in the control spirituality — but is to be practiced and fostered. In this perspective, which we might call surrender spirituality, control is seen as the problem, not the solution.

"Control" and "Surrender" Psychotherapies

Of course these two approaches to spirituality represent two approaches to psychotherapy as well. The control attitude is the dominant mode of psychoanalytically-based approaches — those in which the "demon" of the *id* is postulated.

The attitude of "letting go" and "surrender," on the other hand, is the dominant mode of the experiential psychotherapies, which are themselves rooted in the tradition of humanistic psychology with its belief in the ultimate goodness of the human organism and which thus allows a faith in the ultimate rightness of human processes.

"Hero's Journey" As "Control" Psychotherapy

Since the control attitude, in any of its manifestations, requires the postulation of an ultimate evil against which one must remain vigilant and must fight, the common "hero's journey" myth — with its typical fighting and slaying of supposedly evil parts of the personality and reality symbolized as dragons and other monsters — is a prevalent focal myth to this attitude. Corresponding to this myth are the emphasis on disciplines and practices seeking to develop the ego and the will ... over against the dangers that are postulated to exist in the Universe requiring these disciplines and, so-called, ego developments.

A Different Heroic Response in "Surrender" Paths

Since the "feeling" therapies and the other spiritual and experiential psychotherapeutic modalities with which they are allied are so different in attitude to the traditional "control" attitude, should there not be corresponding differences in myths to exemplify them? Indeed, there are.

In history, the surrender spiritualities have had correspondences in myth in which the dragon is not fought, conquered, and slain, but rather is either tamed and becomes one's ally or pet — Saint Margaret is the prime example in the West, but this is a depiction prevalent in the East — or else one is swallowed by the "dragon" or monster and, after a while, is reborn.

Jonah is the prime example in the West for this latter depiction. But again this reaction to the fearful dissociated aspects of the personality, or the Shadow, is not a common one in the Western patriarchy, and it is much more common in traditional cultures and in the East.

A Shift to "Surrender" As a Corrective to a Western Overweening Ego?

All of this may be changing in recent times in the West, as once again the humanistic attitude and the new spiritual perspectives, as well as the experiential psychotherapies such as primal therapy, make us increasingly aware of the ultimate beneficence of the body, and of the Universe beyond even that, and of the importance of surrender and letting go as a corrective to the overweening control and defensiveness of the diminutive Western ego.

CHAPTER 12

ATMAN PROJECTS VERSUS SURRENDER SOLUTIONS

A Perinatal Flick

A film of postmodern times that is bold with revelation for us is the cult classic, *Nothing but Trouble*, which was released in 1991. It is an especially potent example of the rising pre- and perinatal influence in the media we have been discussing as well as the different heroic response required in these strangest of days because of it. It is all this, plus a twist: As a comedy it represents an unlikely approach to such material and themes. More about that later.

It was produced and written by Peter and Dan Aykroyd and stars Dan Aykroyd, Chevy Chase, Demi Moore, and John Candy. Its reception by modern audiences mirrors exactly the perception in general, to date, that has been had of the perinatal material it depicts so well. For despite the movie's star power and the popularity of its co-creator, Dan Aykroyd, it was met with overwhelmingly negative reviews and received six Razzie nominations, garnering one. I fully expect that until we know better I can expect much the same kind of reaction to this book, because of the perinatal perspective it is revealing of the dark underside of everyday pleasantries and sugar-coated media realities. Yet there is hope for all that we will integrate this hard-to-face yet redemptive material in the fact that the movie does have a strong following among some in our population, just as at present there are some who are not in denial of the bittersweet perinatal vision being revealed.

The Lure Into the Underworld and Call to Adventure

The perinatal adventure of *Nothing but Trouble* begins innocuously with the main characters "leaving the beaten path" on a rather ordinary trip out of the city. Interestingly, the Brazilian couple who have forced themselves on the main characters of Chevy Chase and Demi Moore in making the trip act as impish other-worldly instruments in the change of route.

Joseph Campbell pointed out that the "call to adventure," which marks the beginning of the descent into the transformative nether regions, may be instigated by the merest chance or blunder.[1]

Campbell also writes that the heralds of such a rite of spiritual passage are often loathly and underestimated characters. The Brazilian couple — as gaudy, overbearing, quirky, and from "down under" — perform just this function of luring into the underworld. Thus, they remind us that it is the quirky yet underestimated element in our familiar daily experience that opens us up to the process whose ramifications are huge by comparison.

The Merest Blunder, The Adventure Begins

Sure enough, this innocent-appearing outing is soon disturbed. The merest blunder of map reading results in an ominous tour of an eerie town and its somber and menacing-looking inhabitants. This is followed by a high-speed car chase as the police attempt to pull the innocents over for a bogus traffic violation.

In the tour of the town, it is as if the ego is shown getting a preview or having a precognition of what lies ahead and attempts to flee back into its safe familiar environs. But of course, this emerging piece of unconscious material will not be denied and is able to capture the fleeing ego that we see safely ensconced in its trappings of status and power — symbolized by the BMW with car phone. At this point the main characters, representing the ego, are led, under guard, into the bizarre town of Valkenvania — the encounter with unconscious perinatal begins.

Perinatal Elements

The Junkyard of the Psyche

Campbell says that in the unconscious deep, to which one is beckoned, "are hoarded all the rejected, unadmitted, unrecognized, unknown, or undeveloped factors, laws, and elements of existence."[2]

Likewise, the set in *Nothing But Trouble* is replete with refuse. Bits of history — of rusted and broken refrigerators, automobiles, kitchen appliances, assorted junk, and pieces and parts of all the preceding ... the wreckage of the past — are strewn about as well as heaped in clusters to construct the architecture and delineate the outlines of the drama. The correlation with subconscious remnants of forgotten memories and past emotional experiences is obvious.

Thus the drama evolves in the dumping ground and junkyard of the psyche — where all the rejected tidbits of experience have been relegated.

Stripped of Ego, Perinatal Begins

After being separated from the automobile — that is to say, the ego stripped of defensive trappings of status and worldly position — the characters are rather quickly shuttled into encounters with a myriad of perinatal elements. A few of the obvious ones are as follows:

- Mr. Bonestripper, which is a roller-coaster type ride whose entrance is a large *vagina dentate* mouth that swallows, chews up, and kills. Notice the roller-coaster ride aspect of Mr. Bonestripper, which reflects the emotional extremes and changingness of perinatal, specifically Basic Perinatal Matrix III (BPM III), events.[3]

- The chutes inside the house and of Mr. Bonestripper indicate birth canal symbolism.

- Sexual elements, indicating BPM III influence, are manifest in the scantily clad heroine and the penis-nose of the judge.

- The dark foundry symbolizes the foundation work of the psyche as well as the ominous and eerie aspects of perinatal experience.

- The slave labor surroundings represent similar feelings in the enforced and helpless character of doings just prior to and at the time of birth.

- Notice that the body — the car, the "Beamer" — gets trimmed down, the excess removed, symbolic of the cutting away of past attachments and concerns of a worldly nature, one's "status" reduced.

- Chevy Chase as the main character is at one point forced into a marriage with a huge woman, who is tellingly androgynous in that she is played by John Candy. In her threatening and suffocating embraces we see symbolism of the crushing womb.

- The entire site of these doings is surrounded by a watery trench. This obviously reflects the amniotic surround in the womb.

- Police and guns point to the authoritative character of perinatal doings — in other words, do, or else!

- Death/rebirth symbolism of the perinatal exists in the form of skeletons and huge piles of skulls and bones.

- Scatological, that is to say, fecal symbolism is seen in the "bat-room," which contains an enormous pile of wet bat-shit … excuse the wording, but it really is *shit* and not *feces*.

- The arbitrary nature of justice in the courtroom speaks to that perinatal feeling that one tiny thing, event, or action, has huge and horrifying ramifications.

Big Babies

The most obviously perinatal element, however, is the gargantuan and grotesquely flabby infant twins in diapers. Perinatal feelings are indicated in their extreme crying neediness. Their freshly newborn quality is evident in their fleshiness, which reminds one of the overweight appearance of some newborns, which is usually lost a little later on in infancy. The glossy, waxy sheen on their bodies is reminiscent of the skin of a newborn, which, fresh out of the womb, is wet and slippery, covered in amniotic fluid and cervical mucosa.

A Spiritual Interface

An interesting aspect that indicates the transpersonal, or spiritual, interface with the perinatal is an attic room — a higher mind of memory, kind of like an Akashic record — where all past IDs — identifications — and reports of them — newspaper clippings — are displayed.

Though, interestingly enough, in true perinatal fashion, a macabre lens is used to view these lives — only the reports of their tragic disappearances are seen. I believe that this is a wonderful depiction of how transpersonal information is distorted by perinatal material — the implications of which are far reaching for the pronouncements of so-called spiritual, or psychological, authorities who have not dealt with their perinatal undersides.

Multilevel Feelings

Just When You Thought … .

However an important element in this movie, *Nothing But Trouble*, which is different from artistic representations that deal with only the personal or psychodynamic, is the way the ending opens up under it to a new level, a whole new arena, of issues. Those of us in experiential therapies or breathwork are only too aware of how the perinatal opens up to one, revealing a greater expanse and pervasiveness of dis-ease, at a certain point after dealing with the personal and the psychodynamic.

This layered, or multilevel quality of the movie is shown when the main characters, having heroically escaped through personal effort, find themselves returning to the perinatal realm. Thinking that they have the forces of authority and light on their side, they expect this time to be able to put the evil away once and for all.

But When All Seems Lost … .

To their immense surprise, it appears that the whole world has been conspiring against them — a telling perinatal feeling. The evil is discovered to be pervasive, as if infiltrating every corner of the universe — another perinatal feeling. Even the thoroughly trusted elements of light turn out to be on the side of the darker forces — a vantage point that is part of the hopelessness that characterizes the classic no-exit BPM II scenario. And just like in the womb, then, when all seems lost, something new happens, an explosion or eruption of sorts, which brings down the old world and its structures in a violent conflagration.

Atman Projects Versus Surrender Solutions

This hopeless and futile aspect of the perinatal realms — as opposed to the merely personal or psychodynamic ones — lends itself to its distinctive response — which is surrender, not resistance. Unlike the hero of Campbell's hero's cycle whose task is to slay the dragon using the sword of analytical or cognitive powers, the correct solution here at the perinatal is to let go of all designs, manipulations, and attempts at control and to put oneself into the hands of the seemingly irrational and chaotic Universe, come what may.

How Can You Be Borne Up, If You Won't Let Go?

The Universe's response in the movie — the upsurge of fire from below the earth that brings down the evil structures — demonstrates the theme of being saved by higher forces when one finally is able to surrender. In the same way, in our perinatal experiences, we find ourselves "borne up" and elevated when we once are able to submit to the upsurge of fear-evoking perinatal emotion.

Indeed, when Chevy Chase is seen rolling and setting fire to barrels of oil in a superhuman nick-of-time rescue attempt — in typical "hero's journey" style — I had an odd disjointed sense that we had switched modes. The element seemed incongruous.

Say "Good Night," John Wayne

But, then again, not so. For the movie shows that the successful escape performed through one's own effort is, in actuality, futile. In perinatal terms, such heroics are illusory "atman projects" that ultimately fail against the onslaught of perinatal material, which must be surrendered to, not heroically resisted or conquered.

Interestingly, the eventual surrender solution is echoed earlier on when Chevy Chase is about to go through the chomping jaws of Mr. Bonestripper, the devouring womb. His response, at the prospect of his imminent failure, is to pray — to call on higher forces.

Trusting in Higher Forces

Amazingly, the machine breaks at that moment, signaling the response of such "external" or higher forces. He alone, of all the others who have faced that fate, goes through the machine unscathed. Notice also that he says "Thank you, Lord" afterwards.

Thus it is not on one's own powers that one makes it through perinatal material, rather it is by the relinquishing of such attempts at control and the relying and trusting in higher forces. We are reminded that Dante required the angelic Beatrice to show the way through purgatorio and inferno to paradisio.

The Message

In the next chapter, we will use another postmodern film to expand on these themes. This will allow us to fill out an emerging pattern, as we then compare it with *Nothing But Trouble* and other perinatal evidence.

So let us watch, now, as the pattern, like a photo emerging in solution, reveals to us its features, thus delivering to us the message it has come to bring.

CHAPTER 13

PEACEFUL WARRIORS AND SILLY HEROES

Volcano-Jumping: A Different Heroic Response

This different kind of heroic response — which characterizes the perinatal arena and is sorely needed at this time in history — is exemplified in another contemporary movie of cult status. We will deal with it in some detail to bring out the elements of the kind of hero that is now required to stop the cycles of destruction that have currently driven us to the abyss ... to the very edge of a "volcano."

In *Joe Versus the Volcano*, the main character, played by Tom Hanks, is given a heroic task. But unlike a typical hero's cycle task which stereotypically involves the slaying of a fire-spewing dragon, Joe is asked to give up his life by jumping into a fire-erupting volcano.

The connection between volcano and dragon is that at the second-line or psychodynamic level the fire-spewing aspects of the perinatal, which might be compared to a volcano, can be seen as "embodied" or reduced in the form of a dragon. In the same way, the volcanic energy of perinatal feelings is initially embodied in easier-to-face and "dragonized" psychodynamic, second-line, or childhood traumas and feelings.

You Just Can't Slay a Volcano

But what may *seem* to work at the second-line or psychodynamic level — the conquering or slaying of negative feelings ... and notice that I said "seem" — has no place at all at the perinatal. For here the pain energy is overwhelming and pervasive. Thus the difference is analogous to that between facing the energy of a dragon and facing that of a volcano.

The Heroes We Need — The New Hero's Cycle

First Anima, Then Community

Keep in mind that this movie shows Joe, earlier on, going through all the major stages of the hero's cycle — the retreat from mundane reality, the sailing off into a new and exotic realm of existence and adventure.

It even depicts a typical "dragon slaying" — the hero's conquering of inner fears and risking of one's life for another that results in the uniting with anima energy, that is, the saving of the damsel. So earlier on there is a dealing with psychodynamic energy, just as in *Nothing but Trouble* Chevy Chase deals with psychodynamic material and enacts a dragon slaying by risking his life to rescue Demi Moore from a giant chopping machine. But, also similarly, this results in the opening up of another level, requiring a completely different — indeed, opposite — response. Thus, in *Joe*

Versus the Volcano, Joe is asked to give up his life to save an entire community, not merely to risk his life to rescue his anima, his feeling self.

Risking It All

The ensuing plot has interesting elements as it shows Joe having to decide whether to sacrifice his newly won relationship with his anima ally for the benefit of an entire — but anonymous — community. This demonstrates that at a progressed level of the spiritual process — that having to do with one's inter-connection with the larger community of living things, not just one's personal unconscious — one must risk even one's newly regained creativity, inner child playfulness, and personal feelings, that is to say, one's anima … the damsel.

But in telling fashion, in order to make the higher "community" sacrifice the anima elements that have been let go of, symbolized by Meg Ryan as the anima damsel, end up going with Joe to his chosen fate and are borne up, renewed, along with him.

Borne Up by a Beneficent Universe

On Joe's part, the climax shows the same quality of a beneficent Universe aiding a true and dharmic heart. Joe (with his anima) face what they think is death. Instead they find themselves "borne up" by the volcano, not consumed; and they are deposited (reborn) in a typical perinatal watery surround — the ocean, symbolizing therefore a spiritual birth. This is a perfect depiction of how surrender, not "heroic" resistance, is done and why it needs to be done currently, as I have been pointing out.

"Away From the Things of Man"

In the end, the main characters are floating in the middle of a wide open sea — signifying the immensity of potentiality that is now open, and facing a gigantic moon on the horizon — symbolizing the beneficent nature of the Universe to which they are opening, that is, it is beautiful and lit with possibilities.

They are seen sitting on only their luggage — symbolizing the "stripped down" nature of the self, that is, stripped of ego trappings of status, vainglory, defenses, and so on. Their final comment at the very end of the film is that they do not know where they will end up but only that it will be "away from the things of man" — indicating their desire to never go back to the drama of ego and its puerile catacomb pathways of darkened experience.

The Universe Is You

We see then that in this movie, like *Nothing but Trouble*, the heroic response required is surrender, not resistance or control, and that the response from the Universe is cooperative and helpful, and hardly antagonistic as was feared, especially at earlier levels.

This is in keeping with the discovery at the perinatal, which borders it on the transpersonal, that in fact the Universe, not only is not antagonistic, not only is beneficent and helpful, but in fact is no different from oneself, indeed is oneself … and one begins to wonder why one would ever expect not to be borne up by a Universe that is now seen as inextricably united with one's Self.

Responses to the Perinatal

Returning now to *Nothing But Trouble*, an aspect of it that has significance for dealing with perinatal issues is the way different characters are shown responding to the embodiment of arbitrary justice, the judge. In the wonderfully Kafkaesque courtroom scenes, we see several different types of people — representing different responses to unconscious material — hauled before the judge. The musicians, signifying artists, creative people; the hedonistic criminals; and the main characters, representing average people, each present distinct attitudes, which are responded to differently by the representative of the unconscious, the judge.

Jiving With Your Monsters

The musicians are able to create rhythm and flow. Therefore they are able to get through the experience unharmed. Indeed, they are even able to elicit a response from the judge — getting him to join in. In this way we see how creative people can actually use perinatal material and get it to cooperate for desired ends. We might consider how this relates to the writing of *Nothing but Trouble* itself.

Peter and Dan Aykroyd, in creating this movie, are, like the musicians in the movie, getting the unconscious to "play along," to create something beyond what either the writer or the unconscious could accomplish separately. Much of what is interesting in art is done this way: The deeper fear-evoking material is allowed to come in and enrich, enliven, freshen with new ideas and perspectives, stimulate, and invigorate the creative production.

Beware the Tar Baby

On the other hand, the arrogant banker contends with evil, and, like Brer Rabbit with tar baby, gets stuck.

Notice also that the really contentious ones — the alcoholic drug-using criminal hedonists — are completely lost. Thus the two extremes, as well as the average person are depicted.

Lighten Up!

But the truly striking element that indicates an advanced way of dealing with the perinatal material is shown in the genre of the movie itself. As a comedy, it shows a non-attached and transcendent approach. Chevy Chase and Demi Moore, especially Chevy Chase, show an aloofness and silly playfulness in the face

190

of horror and death that has spiritual implications. Like a Tibetan mystic, Chase refuses to get sucked in to the involved drama confronting him. Like a Christian saint about to be martyred, he jokes, teases, and gets silly with the instruments of horror and evil. Similarly, Demi Moore humors and plays cards with her would-be monsters.

Silly Heroes

Standing within the Witness higher self, they are able to take the entire situation lightly — acting and reacting in the moment to each unique situation as it presents itself. One moment Chevy Chase is confronting his own demise, the next moment he is in a love scene. He alternates a frightful encounter with relaxing and smoking a cigar.

If we want to know what real and transcended behavior is, we might do well to get our hints in the depictions of unattached playfulness — as presented by modern Western actors like Bill Murray, Demi Moore, Tom Hanks, Chevy Chase, Robin Williams, Bruce Willis, and Jim Carrey — rather than in the repressively calmed not-with-it-ness — not-witness — that is sometimes mistaken for spiritual attainment.

Darkening Down

Incidentally, this element of humor shows an entirely different way of dealing with the perinatal than most other movies that deal with this kind of material. The movie, *Brazil*, is a good example of this difference. Not only is *Brazil* cast in an eerie, somber, and tragically hopeless and futile air — indicating that one's response here is to "believe in" the reality of such material — but the only escape in this movie is in a purely conceptual, fantasy way.

The main character cannot face the horror ultimately. He flips out into a reassuring dream sequence brimming with BPM I and BPM IV imagery. Interestingly, reflecting the pattern of progression of our expressions in feeling therapies, the dream includes a BPM III scenario to get him to those later bucolic realms.

But in *Brazil* these are only daydreams. This fact shows a refusal to face this perinatal material or to surrender to it. Rather, in fantasy, one overcomes the horror. It is as if one continues using familiar ego techniques — hero's journey methods, dragon-slaying methods — for dealing with material on a deeper level where they no longer work — where they are in fact counterproductive.

Thus, these techniques can only succeed in dreaming. Terry Gilliam, the creator of *Brazil*, shows us that the hero, in reality, is doomed.

However, one might interpret the main character's escape into fantasy as a victory over evil forces. That the ending lends itself so readily to such an interpretation is a telling indictment of the state of progress of some of us in dealing with perinatal material. Apparently, there are those so lost that the only success possible seems to be in insanity or death.

Evolution In Attitudes to the Perinatal?

However, in *Nothing but Trouble*, the main characters *do* face and deal with all the material. Sometimes they fight it; sometimes run from it; sometimes play with it; sometimes joke, tease, spar, or get silly with it; sometimes are swallowed by it and carried along ... but always they are creatively facing and dealing with it. This different air about and attitude towards the perinatal material can be said to be an advance from the earlier movie, *Brazil*, representing perhaps a progression of our collective consciousness in our attitudes and manner of dealing with the perinatal.

Dancing Above the Dissonance

Such a prospect is, indeed, the auspicious legacy of such a creative project. Though it is doubtful they did so consciously, the Aykroyd brothers and the producers of *Nothing But Trouble* deserve our gratitude for their efforts in lighting forward our collective reality endeavor.

Beyond that, we can take hope in the possibility that Western culture may be rising itself, however minimally at first, above the dramas of light and darkness that have plagued it for so long. The Manichean tendency can lead only to ever-spiraling cycles of resistance and assault. Yet we are seeing currently, not only an erosion of defiantly uni-dimensional ego perspectives, not only a movement toward facing and dealing with our inner darkness, but an integration of opposing forces, a dancing above the *leela* — the play — of light and dark.

The Universality of Divinity Remembered

The perennial understanding of the universality of divinity, both within and without us, in the lowest as well as the highest of places, is the bright at the center of the perinatal bedlam about us. We are guided as well by this gleaming, a rising moon of promise and possibilities.

CHAPTER 14

TO MOVE THE WORLD — A RACE AGAINST TIME

Apocalypse? Or Earth Rebirth?

The Evidence for Change Occurring

Finally it is time to answer the question posed by this book: Apocalypse? Or Earth rebirth? Knowing apocalypse, we can now declare a hearty No! to apocalypse.

Our answer begins by pointing out that we have discovered, in this book, that there are things that can be done to prevent our extinction and, on the contrary, bring in a new dawn of harmonious cooperation with the forces of Nature. In the last five chapters we have seen that there is evidence of a collective change in consciousness occurring. A radical change in our attitudes to war, racism, the environment, and even spirituality — and thus to the very way we live our lives — is manifesting in our culture, the youth of the world, our children, and is even popping up in our collective dreams.

Natural Law

In addition we are aided by some fundamental processes of natural and cosmic law. In preceding chapters I have pointed out how both our nature inside and Nature outside seem to be conspiring to force us into the changes necessary. From this perspective we are in the hands of natural law, and its homeostatic mechanisms may bring us into line in ways unimaginable, beyond even the speculations I put forth in our attempt to see "through Gaia's' eyes" in Chapter Seven.

Visible and Invisible Allies

Furthermore we may be aided by unseen forces and entities of which we know not and may be incapable of knowing. Though I think it foolhardy to sit on our hands and hope that some intergalactic or spiritual cavalry will arrive to save the day at the last moment. Still it is eminently reasonable, considering the minuscule knowledge we have in relation to the immensity of All That Is, to put aside our familiar hubris and at least consider the possibility of aid from higher forces or entities.

Indeed, there are many people in this day and age who believe that particular forces have come together at just this juncture in time to aid us and to ensure our success. Who knows why?

Perhaps it is because our interconnectedness with Everything requires that we not fail, for it would have detrimental effects on things of which we do not know. I must confess that I myself have received knowledge of such help being given us.[1]

Similarly there are others who believe that God will not allow His/Her creation to be destroyed and did indeed come in the flesh to ensure its success.[2]

Cosmic Law

And there may even be cosmic laws at work. "Truth has its own momentum," said one of our workshop participants. My wife and I conducted workshops in what we call *primal breathwork*, which is based on the Holotropic Breathwork™ of Stanislav Grof. In these workshops, which involve access to all aspects of the unconscious, including the spiritual/transpersonal, the biographical-psychodynamic, and the sensory, as well as the perinatal, it is not unusual for us to witness people being motivated, because of their profound transformative experiences, to commit themselves with all their being, talents, and resources, to aid in the processes of renewal on this planet.

But Is It Enough?

Don't Expect to See It on Cable News

But some might argue that there are not enough people changing. You might easily get that impression if your prime source of information is the mainstream media of the cultures of the world. For it is in the interest of the dominant media of all lands to support the status quo — for economic, as well as political reasons. They are not likely to report the new and controversial.

In fact, the proof of this is that when truth is truly democratized and shared freely, as on the Internet, the information that comes out is drastically different from the sanctioned news sources. Indeed, we have seen the social media and the Internet leading in many areas, from Wikileaks to Mideast revolt, everywhere and anywhere. Like a tail wagging a dog, the Internet has been the first to expose information that the controlled media, who knew of it but repressed the information, only afterwards were forced to present.

So don't expect the paid-for media to give you an accurate portrayal of what is truly new and breaking or for them to accurately reflect cultural changes as they occur. And don't either expect for them to present the news of positive developments occurring — especially when those positive developments threaten an entrenched status quo. No, the official information sources of the status quo are the last to report such changes, and they do so only when they absolutely have to.

The Peace Symbol — Moratorium — Reversed

Meanwhile, from my vantage point, I would answer the query that there are not enough people changing by reiterating that, in fact, there are many of us who are integrating this emergent material, who are regaining our truth and the truths of this Earth and the Universe, who are expanding our consciousness to include this information, and who are carrying that information forward into positive action to heal ourselves, the people around us, humanity at large, and the planet.

This response of constructive action is exquisitely expressed when the peace symbol is reversed and symbolizes a human figure with arms upstretched — meaning the expression into the external world of what was discovered within.

Putting Out Our Hand by Creating Healthy Alternatives

An answer to the question of what will happen is that we can hope that the forces of integration are more successful than those of disintegration and reaction in the face of this influx of material, for one thing. In addition, those of us who are dealing positively with these emergent truths can help to build societal structures and processes that make it easier for others less fortunate to face and deal positively with their environmentally enforced psychological transitions.

Those of us who can should put out our hand to our struggling sisters and brothers. If we can set up and provide accessible alternatives to the ones of reaction and acting out that now exist, we are going to make it more likely that those more prone to reaction and avoidance will instead also grow in response to these eco-apocalyptic, bio-noetic changes.

Facing the Monster Is Always Better, Often Beautiful

For, contrary to what many believe, the evidence from the experiential modalities involving the perinatal, and my own experience, concludes that the dangers of not accessing the perinatal unconscious are much greater than the ones of attempting to access them. For our residual birth issues influence us one way or the other. If we deny them, we can be deluded into acting them out, completely unconsciously, without an insight or a clue, in a "fetal trance state," in the form of war, social violence, spouse abuse, sexual promiscuity resulting in the contraction of AIDS, and a myriad of other destructive and self-destructive ways.

Whereas if we turn to face this supposed "monster," with only a tad of insight into these forces that direct our life, we are at least able to avoid the most horrific of the destructive acts that keeping it unconscious can cause us to participate in.

And then, on the more positive side, fully working through these seemingly hellish inner traumas can result in a transformation of the person and a lightness, peace, beauty, and fulfillment of life unlike anything that can be imagined beforehand.

A Race Against Time

Regardless of whether we succeed, we must try. As Stanislav Grof put it in his conclusion to an article on this global crisis: For our very survival,

We seem to be involved in a race for time that has no precedent in the entire history of humanity. What is at stake is nothing less than the future of life on this planet. If we continue the old strategies, which in their consequences are extremely destructive and self-destructive, it is unlikely that the human species will survive. However if a sufficient number of people undergoes a process of deep inner transformation; we might reach a level of consciousness evolution that will bring us to the point of deserving the name given to our species, Home sapiens, *i.e., wise humans.*[3]

"The Leaven In the Dough"

Of course, I do not expect that the sort of application of experiential techniques Grof hopes for above can occur on the massive scale that would seem to be necessary to avoid apocalypse in the short period of time that we have left. Yet it might be that we would be lucky enough for that not to be necessary.

It is possible that simply a significant fraction of the world's population — like the "leaven in the dough" — can make all the difference in the world, literally, by tipping our course one way as opposed to another, especially if these people — because of their healing and their awareness of the crisis — are motivated to place themselves in positions of influence and education, or to put their efforts toward healing, on individual and collective levels, in larger numbers than the average populace would. In other words, not just the leaven in the dough but as persons, standing in the right place and with the lever big enough, who can move the world.

AFTERWORD

CENTAURS, SHAMANS, SACRIFICIAL LAMBS, AND SCAPEGOATS

REFLECTIONS ON A COLLECTIVE SHADOW AND EXPERIENCE AS PRIMARY

I Am You, and You Are Me, and We Are We, and We Are All Together.

DESCRIPTION: *The essence of Christianity is the idea that a person — Jesus Christ, of course, in Christianity — can suffer and die for the "sins" of others, so that those persons won't have to bear the burden of their sins. This article addresses that theme in a larger, multicultural, multi-ethnic, multi-religious context: Are there people who take on the "sins" — or "Pain" — of others, who take on the* karma *— in an Eastern sense — or the mistakes*

200

and evil of others who are not able to handle the consequences of their actions? Is the Divinity inherent in the Cosmos compassionately concerned enough to manifest or call forth individuals to take on the same kind of task that Christ, in a most extreme brutal form, demonstrated? This afterword is not about Christ but about that theme of extraordinary individuals with a divinely-inspired mission of suffering for the sake of others who cannot "help" themselves in raising themselves above the consequences of their ill deeds. For are not people of all times and cultures children of the same Divinity, some would say "sparks" of that same Divinity, which others, including myself, have theorized is commensurate, that is, equal, to all of Nature, including humanity — each and every one of us? Assuming this, in this afterword I discuss this phenomenon of people taking on, willingly and unwillingly, the pain and sins of their society — from the small tribe to that of all of humanity. And I put forth the proposition that there is a collective "pool of pain." In that ultimately the distinctions between people are illusory, that we are all One, all interconnected, then both the evil, as well as the good, of each of us is both the result of the collective actions of us all as well as being a part of the consciousness that we all share — more correctly the One Consciousness that each of us is.

The Community's Inner Dragon

She'd experienced being raped was what she'd told us. This veteran consciousness explorer and trained facilitator had also done a lot of regression work on herself. Yet she related how, in one of her breathwork sessions, she'd definitely had those feelings of rape ... despite the fact that she'd not been sexually abused in this life. And this last part she knew. It was not denial or repression.

The conference attendees were shaken. It did not coincide with any common psychological, or even transpersonal, models concerning healing or experience they'd ever heard of. But in her response, the panelist offered the idea that there is a kind of storehouse of experience of collective pain that anyone can tap-in to, if one is sufficiently open … and ready.

Since this type of thing has come up, as well, in my own inner journeying, I would like to suggest that what we're dealing with is a possibility, based on the evidence, of a sort of *collective shadow unconscious*, a collective pool of pain, if you will, which has been built up currently and in the past of distress that needs to be released.

I remember a Santa Barbara-based spiritual teacher expressed a similar idea. As she put it, after you clear out your own stuff, then you do it for the rest of the species, then for all living beings in this world, then for living things in other worlds, then for all entities, and then so on, and on, and….

Shamans, Sages, Tribal Kings, and Prophets

Similarly, from history, the spiritual literature, and anthropology we hear of certain people — shamans, tribal kings, prophets, saviors, sages, gurus — who, after dealing with their own inner dragons, can tap-in to this collective pool and thereby help other people. In resolving the negative material, releasing it and integrating it, they can have a positive effect on their community, and even the Universe as a whole.

I am reminded of how certain African tribal "kings" (*chieftains* would be a better word), tribal leaders, and "clan kings" would be sacrificed for their tribes to the point of and including actual physical death. Similarly, shamans would take on psychic tasks that they would consider to be too dangerous or difficult for members of their tribe to do. In this way of looking at things, it is as if there is a *group mind*, and that the shaman's duty is to resolve the collective issues, to work through the unfelt feelings, so that the rest of the tribe can function better.

It is as if everyone in a community does not have to, or is not able to, "work" all of their own stuff, but that a certain person can volunteer to face some of those inner demons for the entire group, or at least for those having difficulty.

Ah, But Scapegoats As Well

In this respect I believe it is possible to make a fascinating, albeit disturbing, connection between this idea and scapegoats. In the case of scapegoating, particular individuals are selected to be this kind of lightning rod for the group's pain and psychic distress.

So there seems to be both this tendency for people to adopt this role for themselves and for societies to put people in these roles whether they want it or not. This indicates some kind of social, human need, or at least a fundamental human expediency, that is to say, ego defense.

It would seem, in any case, that there is a right way and wrong way to do this. And we can deduce that these attempts can have either beneficial or negative transpersonal and psychological effects depending on which way it's done. Obviously there is a huge difference between a guru or a savior taking the "sins" of their group upon themselves to release their people in that manner, versus a scapegoat being chosen to dump all the group's unwanted feelings and shadow material on.

Sacrifices — Animal and Cucumber

Other fascinating perspectives on this arise from study of one of its variations: This is the widespread phenomenon of sacrifice, and in particular, animal sacrifice. The Nuer of Africa, for example, as well as the neighboring Dinka, created rituals for many of life's events around the killing of sacrificial oxen. If no oxen were available, a cucumber was often used; in other cultures, lambs or other animals may be used. At any rate, when the ox was slain, the carcass was then split, with one half being consumed and the other half thrown away from them into the bush ... reputedly taking with it the sins, indiscretions, and wayward elements of all those assembled. Higher forces were then called forth and entreated to remove the carcass/transgressions; indeed, at times they were directly invoked, then subsequently admonished to "go away" and "be gone!"

Since the group or individual is said to be identified with the animal, it is interesting to consider the possible message here that one takes into oneself and *incorporates* (integrates) only half of that which is of oneself; but one seeks the Universe's help in disposing of the other half, relegating it to "the bush." It is fascinating to think of the common use of prayer in this respect, that is, prayer where one invokes the Divine to take away or to "handle" those things in life, or the parts of those things, that one is incapable of handling oneself. Apparently it is the rare individual who completely integrates her or his Shadow.

Experience Is Primary

It is important to keep in mind that all of this idea of a group psyche is built upon a perspective, a paradigm, in which subjectivity is primary: Experience or Mind being the only reality. Such speculation as engaged in here is not even conceivable within the dominant materialistic paradigm. Nevertheless, these possibilities have long ... far longer than this upstart of "objective materialism" has been around ... have long been the common currency of our species, and have been so in the vast majority of human cultures that ever existed.

Shared Experience: Morphic Resonances and COEX Systems

But, getting back to the subject, people having rape fantasies, both men and women, where apparently there has been no sexual abuse, is becoming ever more common. Is it that in some way when we are violated as children, *psychologically and emotionally*, that it's part of a gestalt or resonance — Stanislav Grof would say a *COEX system*; Rupert Sheldrake would say a *morphogenetic field* or *morphic resonance* — that includes actual *physical* violations from a collective pool of pain?

Also we should consider all the current stories of people being sexually abused; there seems to be an epidemic of people claiming to have been sexually molested as *infants* by their parents. No doubt much of this is true. The evidence is there to confirm it. But is it also possible that people in processing their stuff, or coming close to their repressed feelings, are at times tapping into transpersonal resonances that are only similar in quality to the corresponding real-life trauma? This is a possibility we should consider; for I know it to be the only plausible one in my own case, in the case of the panelist mentioned at the outset , and in the cases of several others whom I know personally or whose cases have appeared in print.

UFOs: Is That Gaia Calling?

Another item related to this pattern is the current UFO abduction experiences — the incidence of which is also increasing. One interesting explanation for such experiences of being abducted and then examined, probed, and sampled — which corresponds to this collective pool of pain theory — is derived from the idea that in fact the Earth herself (Gaia) has consciousness and is therefore part of a collective consciousness to which we also belong. This idea of an earth hologram is propounded by Goddess theorists and by others as well. Joseph Chilton Pearce claims we have primary access to such an Earth hologram as children and lose it later through our normative indoctrination into society.

He writes:

The brain as a hologram is representative of the Earth. So long as this is undifferentiated, the personality, or consciousness within that brain, receiving its perceptions from that brain, is literally an undifferentiated part of the hologram effect. It is part and parcel of the world system, which, because it radiates out from the child, places him at the center of thought, with the world a body extending from him. The clarification of the hologram (to use that model) is a period of breathless wonder and excitement for the child because he is discovering his larger self. . . .

The primary process is the function through which we are conscious of the Earth as a thinking globe, the flow of life, the general field of awareness, and almost surely, even larger ecologies of thought. The primary process is also past, current, and potential possibility and experience. Other cultures have maintained a much greater openness to the primary process than Western culture has. . . .

Nevertheless, the potential for access to this "primary process" always exists, since it is repressed but continues to exist in the unconscious.

With these things in mind, is it possible that UFO abductees may be inadvertently stumbling into primary Earth process and picking up on the feelings of Earth herself as she is being poked, violated, measured, and having things inserted into her in this modern, high-tech, resource-exploiting era.

If so, one has to wonder whether some of the feelings of the Earth herself might not be being expressed *or be trying to be integrated by her through these people*. Is it possible that these people have become unwitting channels for Mother Earth's pain — to help to express and integrate it — as she is systematically being defoliated, polluted, violated, and destroyed?

This may sound farfetched, but then, considering our actions in the face of global disaster ... well, so are the times! Furthermore, I helped facilitate at least one inner journeyer whose experience was exactly this. Her interpretation of the powerful experience my wife and I both witnessed was that she was feeling and releasing pain and distress of all women throughout history and then Mother Earth herself. What gave extra credibility to her experience for me was that I observed what looked like her experiencing the pain of women in birth. Yet, like the rape reliving that was not of this life, this woman had never given birth herself ... not in this life, anyway.

Volcano-Jumping for Bliss and Profit

Anyway, I offer these speculations in the hope of stimulating renewed appreciation of the roles as journeyers and shamans — as they have reemerged in their modern form in the deep experiential growth modalities such as holotropic breathwork and primal therapy, both of which I have substantial experience with. It may just be that what we do on our "inner" forays into consciousness has significance in the "outer" world — in these incredibly delicate and precipitous times — far beyond what we normally think. Indeed we may be volunteering for an ancient role, and in these days, perhaps, a very much needed one. Like Joe in the Tom Hanks movie, *Joe Versus the Volcano*, we may find ourselves "jumping into the volcano to save the community." But also like Joe, and my experience attests to this, I believe we will find that the Universe provides, not death, but rather bears up and rewards with renewed life those who voluntarily sacrifice themselves this way.

NOTES

Chapter One

1. *Stop, Children, What's That Sound — Buffalo Springfield —*
Lyrics
There's something happening here
What it is ain't exactly clear
There's a man with a gun over there
Telling me i got to beware

I think it's time we stop, children, what's that sound
Everybody look what's going down

There's battle lines being drawn
Nobody's right if everybody's wrong
Young people speaking their minds
Getting so much resistance from behind

I think it's time we stop, hey, what's that sound
Everybody look what's going down

What a field-day for the heat
A thousand people in the street
Singing songs and carrying signs
Mostly say, hooray for our side

It's time we stop, hey, what's that sound
Everybody look what's going down

Paranoia strikes deep
Into your life it will creep
It starts when you're always afraid
You step out of line, the man come and take you away

We better stop, hey, what's that sound
Everybody look what's going down
Stop, hey, what's that sound
Everybody look what's going down
Stop, now, what's that sound
Everybody look what's going down
Stop, children, what's that sound
Everybody look what's going down

2. It's the End of the World as We Know It — R.E.M. — Lyrics

That's great, it starts with an earthquake, birds,
snakes, an aeroplanes, Lenny Bruce is not afraid.
Eye of a hurricane, listen to yourself churn — world
serves its own needs, dummy serve your own needs. Feed
it off an aux speak, grunt, no, strength, Ladder
start to clatter with fear fight down height. Wire
in a fire, representing seven games, a government
for hire and a combat site. Left of west and coming in
a hurry with the furies breathing down your neck. Team
by team reporters baffled, trumped, tethered cropped.
Look at that low playing! Fine, then. Uh oh,
overflow, population, common food, but it'll do. Save

yourself, serve yourself. World serves its own needs,
listen to your heart bleed dummy with the rapture and
the revered and the right, right. You vitriolic,
patriotic, slam, fight, bright light, feeling pretty
psyched.

[Chorus:]

It's the end of the world as we know it.
It's the end of the world as we know it.
It's the end of the world as we know it, and I feel fine.

Six o'clock — TV hour. Don't get caught in foreign
towers. Slash and burn, return, listen to yourself
churn. Locking in, uniforming, book burning, blood
letting. Every motive escalate. Automotive incinerate.
Light a votive, light a candle. Step down, step down.
Watch your heel crush, crushed, uh-oh, this means no
fear cavalier. Renegade steer clear! A tournament,
tournament, a tournament of lies. Offer me solutions,
offer me alternatives and I decline.

[Chorus 2x]

The other night I dreamt of knives, continental
drift divide. Mountains sit in a line, Leonard
Bernstein. Leonid Brezhnev, Lenny Bruce and Lester
Bangs. Birthday party, cheesecake, jelly bean, boom! You
symbiotic, patriotic, slam book neck, right? Right.

[Chorus 2x]

3. *Break on Through to the Other Side — The Doors — Lyrics*
You know the day destroys the night,
Night divides the day
Tried to run, tried to hide,

Break on through to the other side,
Break on through to the other side,
Break on through to the other side, yeah.

We chased our pleasures here,
Dug our treasures there,
But can you still recall the time we cried?
Break on through to the other side,
Break on through to the other side.

Yeah!
C'mon, yeah.

Everybody loves my baby,
Everybody loves my baby.
She gets
She gets
She gets
She gets higghhhh!

I found an island in your arms,
A country in your eyes,
Arms that chained us, eyes that lied.
Break on through to the other side,
Break on through to the other side,
Break on through, wow, oh yeah!

Made the scene week to week,
Day to day, hour to hour,
The gate is straight, deep and wide,
Break on through to the other side,
Break on through to the other side,
Break on through,
Break on through,
Break on through,
Break on through,

Break, break, break, break,
Break, break, break, break,
Break.

4. U.R.A. Fever — The Kills — Lyrics

Walk you to the counter
What do you got to offer
Pick you out a solder
Look at you forever
Walk you to the water
Your eyes like a casino
We ain't born typical
Find a piece of silver
Pretty as a diagram
And go down to the Rio
Put it in my left hand
Put it in a fruit machine
Everyone's a winner
Laughing like a seagull
You are a fever
You are a fever
You ain't born typical
You are a fever
You are a fever
You ain't born typical
Living in a suitcase
Meet a clown, fall in love
went down to have you over
Going 'round a break up
Take you to a jukebox
That's the situation
Pick you out a number
And that's our arrangement
Dancing on the legs of a new-born pony

Left right left right
Keep it up son
Go ahead and have her
Go ahead and leave her
You only ever had her
When you were a fever
I am a fever
I am a fever
I ain't born typical
I am a fever
I am a fever
I ain't born typical
We are a fever
We are a fever
We ain't born typical
We are a fever
We are a fever
We ain't born typical
We are a fever
We are a fever
We ain't born typical
We are a fever
We are a fever
We ain't born typical

5. "If the bees disappeared, then man would only have four years of life left. No more bees, no more pollination, no more plants, no more animals, no more man." — Albert Einstein

Vanishing bees is "just a sign" of what is going on. The canary has died, and we cannot just leave the coal mine.

6. Gulf Oil Spill, Fukushima meltdowns, nuclear radiation, toxic nuclear waste, HAARP, killing off of the ocean — destroying oxygen in it, dead zones with no oxygen, dolphins washing up,

birds falling out of the sky, bees disappearing, ozone depletion at the rate of 40% in a recent two months alone, and a massive 50% species extinction in the next few decades, that is to say, *in our lifetimes*! (now, enjoy your hamburger.)

7. Helen Caldicott compares our complacency in the face of these dire happenings to the parents who respond emotionless when she has to tell them their child has leukemia. She says, "Get mad. Get emotional." She urges us to take back our governments from these mad perpetrators of the darkest doom imaginable. And, in the least, occupy! She proclaims,

It's time you took your country back.... Use your bodies like they did in Wisconsin. Do a Tahrir Square here. Take back New York. Take back the Congress. Invade the Congress! Those people belong to you. They are your representatives, and you are their leaders. But you've got to have some guts! And stop being so goddamn polite all the time! And don't need approval. Step up to the plate ... .

We've got to be emotional.... It's time we used our emotions and become incensed! Otherwise we're not going to make it.

8. "We're all gonna fry." With appreciation to Scout Niblett, "We're All Gonna Die/ Your Beat Kicks Back Like Death"

9. "We Lost 40% of Ozone Layer Last 3 Months" proclaimed CNN in April, 2011 — "Ozone Depletion Over Arctic 'Unprecedented' This Winter"

My take on this: CNN reported this month that 40% of the ozone layer over the Arctic was depleted from December 21st, 2010 to March 31st, 2011 — roughly three months. I heard a CNN anchor report this, with some alarm. I also watched as this anchor continued, after a few sentences on this, to another news item — about a snake getting loose in New York, if memory serves me. Guess life on this planet not as big a deal.

By the way, if you want to dismiss this by consoling yourself that it is "only" happening over the Arctic, consider what is happening in parts of the globe that aren't being actively monitored. Seems to me if the lake goes down on the other side, the water is lower on my side as well.

10. John Leslie, *The End of the World.*

Chapter Two

1. Chapter titled with appreciation and admiration to The Kills for their recording, U R A Fever. The lyrics go, "I am a fever, you are a fever, we ain't born typical...." and so on. The music video produced is similarly brilliant. Together, it is a production bordering on genius. The video contains levels of meaning that are only obvious on subsequent viewings.

2. In the *Pre- and Perinatal Psychology Newsletter* I was applauded for being the first person in the United States to teach the subject of pre- and perinatal psychology at the university level and — as it was said, remarkably — for doing it while still a student. I did this at Sonoma State University, in Rohnert Park, California, in the years 1994 and 1995, beginning while I was a graduate student there.

My graduate thesis became the book, *Falls From Grace: Spiritual and Philosophical Perspectives of Prenatal and Primal Experience*, which is listed in Wikipedia as a reference under the topic of *prenatal and perinatal psychology.*

Subsequently, I became the editor of the professional journal, *Primal Renaissance: The Journal of Primal Psychology*, formerly published by the International Primal Association. Much of the contents of its issues were later posted to my website, *Primal Spirit*, where they can still be viewed.

I have had my writings published in *The Journal of Psychohistory*, including some that later became part of this book. In fact, I presented the material of this book originally at an Institute for Psychohistory Association convention; and its earliest publications were in *The Journal of Psychohistory* under the title, "The Scenery of Healing: Commentary On DeMause's 'Restaging Prenatal and Birth Trauma's in War and Social Violence'" *23*/4, 395-405.

These are among my many credentials in this field of pre- and perinatal psychology, where I have studied and trained from 1972 till this day.

3. Stanislav Grof, *Realms of the Human Unconscious: Observations from LSD Research*. New York: Viking Press, 1975; *LSD Psychotherapy*. Pomona, CA: Hunter House, 1980; *Beyond the Brain: Birth, Death, and Transcendence in Psychotherapy*. Albany, NY: State University of New York Press, 1985; *The Adventure of Self-Discovery: Dimensions of Consciousness and New Perspectives in Psychotherapy and Inner Exploration*. Albany, NY: State University of New York Press, 1988; *The Holotropic Mind: The Three Levels of Human Consciousness and How They Shape Our Lives*. San Francisco: HarperSanFrancisco, 1993.

4. Lloyd deMause, "Restaging Early Traumas in War and Social Violence." *The Journal of Psychohistory 23* (1995): 344-391. (Reprinted, with permission, on the *Primal Spirit* website as "Restaging Prenatal and Birth Traumas in War and Social Violence")

Chapter Three

1. For an analysis of the pre- and perinatal elements of "Independence Day," see Anne Marquez's article on the *Primal Spirit* website: "'Independence Day': Pre- and Perinatal Adventure in Film."

2. The text for "Birthing, Forgetting" can be found at "My Beginning, At Least the Part Anyone Could See: Birthing … Forgetting (a short story)" on my site, *SillyMickel Adzema's Life — Autobiography*. It was originally published in — Michael D. Adzema, "Birthing, Forgetting (a story)." *Primal Renaissance: The Journal of Primal Psychology*, 2(1), Spring 1996, pp. 65-76

3. See Stanislav Grof on this at "Planetary Survival and Consciousness Evolution: Psychological Roots of Human Violence and Greed" on the *Primal Spirit* website.

Chapter Four

1. Alvin H. Lawson, "UFO abductions or birth memories?" *Fate, 38*(3) March 1985, pp. 68-80; and Alvin H. Lawson, "Perinatal imagery in UFO abduction reports." In T. Verny (ed.): *Pre- and Perinatal Psychology: An Introduction*. Human Sciences Press, New York, 1987.

2. Alvin H. Lawson, "Placental Guitars, Umbilical Mikes, and the Maternal Rock-Beat: Birth Fantasies and Rock Music Videos." *The Journal of Psychohistory 21* (1994): 335-353.

3. Daniela F. Mayr & Artur R. Boelderl, "The Pacifier Craze: Collective Regression in Europe." *The Journal of Psychohistory 21* (1993): 143-156.

4. This obvious though insistently overlooked fact has scientific support, of course:

According to a study conducted by scientists from the Scripps Institute there is less oxygen in the atmosphere today than there used to be. The ongoing study, which accumulated and interpreted data from NOAA monitoring stations all over the world, has been running from 1989 to the present. It monitored both the rise of carbon dioxide in the atmosphere and the decline in oxygen. The conclusion of that 20 year study is that, as carbon dioxide (produced primarily by burning fossil fuels) accumulates in the atmosphere, available oxygen is decreasing.

Carbon dioxide seems to be almost the total focus of attention in the climate change model as it exists today. After reviewing the results of this study and talking with Dr. Ralph Keeling (one of the lead scientists on the study), it seemed to me that the consequences of atmospheric oxygen depletion should be included in any discussion of atmospheric change ... .

Read more: "Atmospheric Oxygen Levels Fall as Carbon Dioxide Rises" at http://blogcritics.org/scitech/article/atmospheric-oxygen-levels-fall-as-carbon/#ixzz1ru2460V8

5. A. Briend, "Fetal Malnutrition: The Price of Upright Posture?" *British Medical Journal 2* (1979): 317-319.

6. See my blog/book *Culture War, Class War*, especially "Chapter Two: Matrix Aroused, the Sixties" and "Chapter Four: Drugs and Generations — Concocted Worlds" and "Chapter Five: The King Won't Die — An Aborted Changing of the Guard." These are available online as well as in print in my book, *Culture War, Class War,* which is being published simultaneously with this one.

7. These aspects and generational phenomena are spelled out in more detail in my work-in-progress, *Regression, Mysticism, and "My Generation."* Right at hand, however, you can read an elaboration of some of these ideas in the chapters mentioned in *Culture War, Class War* — especially Chapters One through Seven and the post, "Awakening Millennial Generation Occupy Global Revolution." These are available online as well as in print in my book, *Culture War, Class War,* which is being published simultaneously with this one.

8. "Culture War, Class War Chapter Three: Drugs and Generations — Opposing Worlds." Again, this is available online as well as in

print in my book, *Culture War, Class War,* which is being published simultaneously with this one.

Chapter Five

1. Stanislav Grof, "Planetary Survival and Consciousness Evolution: Psychological Roots of Human Violence and Greed." *Primal Renaissance: The Journal of Primal Psychology* 2(1): 3-26, p. 23. Article reprinted, with permission, on *Primal Spirit* site.

2. See Solter, Aletha, (1996), "Tears For Trauma: Birth Trauma, Crying, and Child Abuse" on *Primal Spirit* website on how birth trauma sometimes contributes to and/or triggers child abuse.

3. For an at-hand description of DeMause's psychogenic modes see "The History of Childhood As The History of Child Abuse."on the Primal Spirit site and in print.

Chapter Six

1. "Zombie" by the Cranberries lyrics:

Another head hangs lowly
Time is slowly taken
And the violence causes silence
Who are we mistaken?
Let he see, it's not me
It's not my family
In your head, in your head
They are fightin!
With their tanks, and their bombs
And their bombs, and their guns
In your head, in your head
They are cryin!

In your head! In your head!
Zombie! Zombie! Zombie!
Whats in your head, in your head?
Zombie! Zombie! Zombie!
Another mother's breaking
Heart is taken over.
When the violence causes silence
We must be mistaken.
It's the same old theme
Since 1916!
In your head, in your head
They're still fightin!
With their tanks, and their bombs
And their bombs, and their guns
In your head, in your head!
They are dyin!
In your head! In your head!
Zombie! Zombie! Zombie!
What's in your head, in your head?
Zombie! Zombie! Zombie!

2. Alice Miller, *For Your Own Good*. New York: Farrar, Straus and Giroux, 1984; and Lloyd deMause, "Restaging Early Traumas in War and Social Violence." *The Journal of Psychohistory 23* (1995): 344-391. (Reprinted, with permission, on *Primal Spirit* site as "Restaging Prenatal and Birth Traumas in War and Social Violence")

3. Stanislav Grof, "Planetary Survival and Consciousness Evolution: Psychological Roots of Human Violence and Greed." *Primal Renaissance: The Journal of Primal Psychology 2*(1): 3-26, p. 23. (Article reprinted, with permission, on this *Primal Spirit* website).

4. See "It's the Attack on Privacy, Stupid! What Republicans and

Pundits Don't Get About Clinton's Support," on the Primal Spirit site, for more on the angry electorate and how it played out in the 1996 election.

5. Lloyd deMause, *The Foundations of Psychohistory*. New York: Creative Roots, 1982, p. 139. See also "Are Some 'Sick' People More Healthy Than Normals?"

6. See also "Are Some 'Sick' People More Healthy Than Normals?" on the *Primal Spirit* site.

7. Lloyd deMause, *The Foundations of Psychohistory*. New York: Creative Roots, 1982, p. 143.

Chapter Seven

1. "This Land Is Your Land" is most often used as a form of feel good jingoism and heart-swelling expression of love of the homeland.

But this defense of the Fatherland is also, rather pathetically, a feel good denial and a counter to the reality of what we are doing to our land and our country in the US. The lyrics, as Woody Guthrie wrote them, are indeed anything but jingoistic.

The same thing has happened with Bruce Springstein's "Born In the USA," by the way, where a critique of the Fatherland has become a patriotic anthem by ignoring most of the lyrics except the ironic chorus. It has been harder to distort the meaning of John Mellencamp's "Little Pink Houses," thankfully.

Anyway, here is the unsanitized version of Woody Guthrie's sarcastic "anthem."

This land is your land, this land is my land

From California to the New York Island
From the Redwood Forest to the Gulf Stream waters
This land was made for you and me.
As I went walking that ribbon of highway
I saw above me that endless skyway
I saw below me that golden valley
This land was made for you and me.
I roamed and I rambled and I followed my footsteps
To the sparkling sands of her diamond deserts
While all around me a voice was sounding
This land was made for you and me.
When the sun came shining, and I was strolling
And the wheat fields waving and the dust clouds rolling
A voice was chanting, As the fog was lifting,
This land was made for you and me.
This land is your land, this land is my land
From California to the New York Island
From the Redwood Forest to the Gulf Stream waters
This land was made for you and me.
There was a big high wall there that tried to stop me;
Sign was painted, it said private property;
But on the back side it didn't say nothing;
This land was made for you and me.

Woody Guthrie has a variant:

As I went walking I saw a sign there
And on the sign it said "No Trespassing.
"But on the other side it didn't say nothing,
That side was made for you and me.

It also has a verse:

Nobody living can ever stop me,
As I go walking that freedom highway;

Nobody living can ever make me turn back
This land was made for you and me.

In the squares of the city, In the shadow of a steeple;
By the relief office, I'd seen my people.
As they stood there hungry, I stood there asking,
Is this land made for you and me?

From Wikipedia, *"This Land Is Your Land"*

2. See also "Are Some 'Sick' People More Healthy Than Normals?" on the *Primal Spirit* site.

Chapter Eight

1. The book mentioned was posted online in two places in August, 2011: the websites, Culture War; and Culture War, Class War. *Culture War, Class War: Occupy Generations and The Rise and Fall of "Obvious Truths"* is now also available in print and as an e-book, as it is being published simultaneously with this one.

2. Lloyd deMause, "Restaging of Early Traumas in War and Social Violence." *The Journal of Psychohistory 23* (1995): 2. Reprinted with permission on the *Primal Spirit* site.

Stanislav Grof, *Realms of the Human Unconscious: Observations from LSD Research*. New York: Viking Press, 1975; *LSD Psychotherapy*. Pomona, CA: Hunter House, 1980; *Beyond the Brain: Birth, Death, and Transcendence in Psychotherapy*. Albany, NY: State University of New York Press, 1985; *The Adventure of Self-Discovery: Dimensions of Consciousness and New Perspectives in Psychotherapy and Inner Exploration*. Albany, NY: State University of New York Press, 1988; *The Holotropic Mind: The Three Levels of Human Consciousness and How They Shape Our Lives*. San Francisco: HarperSanFrancisco, 1993.

3. I explain this in more detail in "Chapter Two: We Ain't Born Typical" under the heading "Elements of Birth Experience."

4. "You'll wallow in the shit and you'll think you're happy" and "You're really in a laundry room" from, and with appreciation to, Kurt Cobain. These are lyrics in his song, "Sad." The video and lyrics are reproduced again here for your convenience:

Nirvana — "Sad" (also "Sappy" and "Verse Chorus Verse") — Lyrics

And if you save yourself You will make him happy
He'll keep you in a jar And you'll think you're happy
He'll give you breathing holes Then you'll think you're happy
He'll cover you with grass And you'll think you're happy Now
You're really in a laundry room, You're really in a laundry room
Conclusion came to you, oh

And if you cut yourself You will think you're happy
He'll keep you in a jar Then you'll make him happy
He'll give you breathing holes Then you'll think you're happy
He'll cover you with grass Then you'll think you're happy Now
You're really in a laundry room, You're really in a laundry room
Conclusion came to you, oh (x2)

And if you fool yourself You will make him happy
He'll keep you in a jar And you'll think you're happy
He'll give you breathing holes Then you will seem happy
You'll wallow in your shit Then you'll think you're happy Now
You're really in a laundry room (x3)
Conclusion came to you, oh

Alternate lyrics:

And if you kill yourself You will make him happy

5. Lloyd deMause, "Restaging of Early Traumas in War and Social Violence." *The Journal of Psychohistory 23* (1995): 2. Reprinted with permission on the *Primal Spirit* site.

Stanislav Grof, *Realms of the Human Unconscious: Observations from LSD Research.* New York: Viking Press, 1975; *LSD Psychotherapy.* Pomona, CA: Hunter House, 1980; *Beyond the Brain: Birth, Death, and Transcendence in Psychotherapy.* Albany, NY: State University of New York Press, 1985; *The Adventure of Self-Discovery: Dimensions of Consciousness and New Perspectives in Psychotherapy and Inner Exploration.* Albany, NY: State University of New York Press, 1988; *The Holotropic Mind: The Three Levels of Human Consciousness and How They Shape Our Lives.* San Francisco: HarperSanFrancisco, 1993.

6. "Stand in the place where you are ... just stand" from and with appreciation to R.E.M. While it seems no one understood the group's huge initial release, "Stand," it is quite meaningful in the current context. A video and lyrics are included here for your consideration:

R.E.M. — "Stand" ... lyrics

Stand in the place where you live
Now face North
Think about direction
Wonder why you haven't before
Now stand in the place where you work
Now face West
Think about the place where you live
Wonder why you haven't before
If you are confused check with the sun
Carry a compass to help you along
Your feet are going to be on the ground
Your head is there to move you around

[repeat 1st verse]
Your feet are going to be on the ground
Your head is there to move you around
If wishes were trees the trees would be falling
Listen to reason
Season is calling
[repeat 1st verse]
If wishes were trees the trees would be falling
Listen to reason
Reason is calling
Your feet are going to be on the ground
Your head is there to move you around
So Stand (stand)
Now face North
Think about direction, wonder why you haven't before
Now stand (stand)
Now face West
Think about the place where you live
Wonder why you haven't
[repeat 1st verse]
Stand in the place where you are (Now face North)
Stand in the place where you are (Now face West)
Your feet are going to be on the ground (Stand in the place where you are)
Your head is there to move you around, so stand.

Chapter Nine

1. A. Briend, "Fetal Malnutrition: The Price of Upright Posture?" *British Medical Journal 2* (1979): 317-319.

2. DeMause, op. cit., 1995, p. 12, emphasis in original.

3. See, for example, Alice Miller, *For Your Own Good: Hidden Cruelty in Child-Rearing and the Roots of Violence*, trans. by Hildegarde and Hunter Hannum. New York: Farrar, Straus and Giroux, especially "Vantage Point 1990," pp. vii-ix.

4. Daniela F. Mayr & Artur R. Boelderl, "The Pacifier Craze: Collective Regression in Europe." *The Journal of Psychohistory 21* (1993): 143-156.

5. *Ibid.*, p. 144.

6. *Ibid.*, p. 148, emphasis mine.

7. *Ibid.*, pp. 149-150.

8. Regarding the "experiential," I should make clear that this approach is, from the perspective of the experiential psychotherapeutic approach I will be describing shortly, actually the superficial symbolic acting out of these underlying and powerful cycles in a way that is only a little less impotent than the Freudians.

9. DeMause, op. cit., 1995.

10. Alvin H. Lawson, "Placental Guitars, Umbilical Mikes, and the Maternal Rock-Beat: Birth Fantasies and Rock Music Videos." *The Journal of Psychohistory 21* (1994): 335-353.

11. Mayr and Boelderl claim quite wrongly and quite strangely — as if to make the facts not conflict with deMause's psychogenic theory, or as if to cover up some hole in their analysis — that those caught up in the pacifier craze were raised under the intrusive and socializing parenting modes (op. cit., 1993, p. 145) and yet, in 1992, were between the ages of 15 and 30 (Ibid., p. 143). This is hard to understand because these youth would have been born between the years 1962 and 1977 in advanced Western countries of

mostly Western Europe — Italy, Germany, Austria, all of Europe, and even the U.S. (Ibid.).

However, the intrusive and socializing modes are associated, by deMause, with the eighteenth century and the nineteenth to mid-twentieth centuries, respectively, in the Western world (deMause, op. cit., 1982, p. 62). On the other hand, the helping mode begins mid-twentieth century in the Western world (Ibid., p. 63).

The conclusion from this is that these youth, described by Mayr and Boelderl, would have been greatly influenced by the helping mode. They would be expected, at least, to have received the most advanced methods of child-caring overall in the world at this time — considering deMause's theory — since they are the most recent progeny of the Western world!

Indeed, if these cannot be considered products of the helping mode, who can be? In order for Mayr and Boelderl to dispute this and claim they were exceptions to the rule and were raised under intrusive and socializing modes, they would have had to do a study demonstrating this, or at least cite one done. And this they do not do.

12. Michael D. Adzema, "Reunion With the Positive (Self), Part 1: The Other Half of 'The Cure.'" *Primal Renaissance: The Journal of Primal Psychology* 1(2): 72-85. Reprinted on the *Primal Spirit* site.

13. Arthur Janov, *The Primal Scream: Primal Therapy: The Cure for Neurosis*. New York: Dell, 1970.

14. Ibid.

15. Glenn Davis, *Childhood and History in America*. New York: The Psychohistory Press, 1976.

16. Ibid., especially Ch. 7, "The Great Society and the Youth Revolt," and p. 240.

17. Ibid.

18.Ibid., p. 241.

19. Kenneth Keniston, *The Uncommitted: Alienated Youth in American Society*. New York: Dell, 1965; *Young Radicals: Notes on Committed Youth*. New York: Harcourt, Brace & World, Inc., 1968.

20. While these aspects of youth are laid out by Keniston, a fuller delineation of these dynamics are to be seen in my work-in-progress, tentatively titled *The Once and Current Generation: "Regression," Mysticism, and "My Generation."* [Stay tuned.]

Chapter Ten

1. For "overexamined life,"see Keniston, op. cit., 1965; for "psychological-mindedness" and "self-analysis" see Keniston, op. cit., 1968, especially p. 81.

2. Davis, op. cit., especially Ch. 7, "The Great Society and The Youth Revolt."

3. Mayr and Boelderl, op. cit., p. 149.

Chapter Eleven

1. See especially Ken Wilber, *The Atman Project*. Wheaton, IL: Theosophical Publishing House, 1980.

2. See, for example, Michael Adzema, "A Primal Perspective on Spirituality," *Journal of Humanistic Psychology*, 25(3), 83-116. Reprinted online at the *Primal Spirit* site at *"A Primal Perspective on Spirituality."*

Chapter Twelve

1. Joseph Campbell, *The Hero With a Thousand Faces*. Princeton, NJ: Princeton University Press, 1968, p. 51.

2. Ibid., p. 52.

3. As a reminder, BPM III events (Basic Perinatal Matrix III events), using the typology set forth by Stanislav Grof in his many works, are the events surrounding the actual birth struggle of the infant during delivery. These parts on the perinatal in film make mention also of BPM II, which is related to the time of severe compression and constriction of the fetus in the latter stages of pregnancy and prior to the actual onset of delivery — which are characterized by feelings of "no-exit"; of BPM IV, which is concerned with the feelings of release, triumph, being saved, and whatever else occurs immediately after delivery; and of BPM I, which is related to the state of the fetus earlier in pregnancy — prior to compression — which is often conceived to have "oceanic" and "blissful" qualities, though not always.

Chapter Fourteen

1. See "Some Cosmic Encouragement: I Was Told "Once There Lived 'Noble' Beings" and Now Is the Time for a Regeneration of Peoples to Regain What We Lost," which is the prologue of a book that expands on and goes even deeper into the themes of this one. My *Wounded Deer and Centaurs* is available online now and is to be published in 2014.

2. See "Sathya Sai Baba, Avatar" by Mary Lynn Adzema, on the *Primal Spirit* site.

3. Stanislav Grof, "Planetary Survival and Consciousness Evolution: Psychological Roots of Human Violence and Greed." *Primal Renaissance: The Journal of Primal Psychology* 2(1): 3-26, p. 25. Article reprinted, with permission, on *Primal Spirit* site.

ABOUT THE AUTHOR

I have taught, trained, and facilitated in the fields of primal therapy, holotropic breathwork, rebirthing, and prenatal and perinatal psychology. I was the first person in the United States to teach Prenatal and Perinatal Psychology at the university level, at Sonoma State University, Rohnert Park, California, in the early Nineties. My research and experience have convinced me that the perspective that this kind of deep understanding brings to personal growth and spirituality are nothing short of revolutionary.

My forty-five years of research in this field has convinced me that the time before birth is the unknown puzzle piece in the old paradigm and the key to the new one. It brings it all together in a new zeitgeist, a new comprehension and vision, as sweeping as the one that changed with the discovery of the Earth's true shape. It is the next frontier in evolution ... and the only one separating us from liberation ... and from saving the planet and stopping war and greed.

My name is Michael Adzema. I am a writer, independent scholar, primal therapist, breathwork facilitator, and political activist. My expertise is in the fields of prenatal and perinatal psychology, primal psychology, psychohistory, psychological anthropology, and humanistic psychology. I have done considerable work in these fields as well: history, economics, anthropology, and environmental studies. I have studied extensively in the fields of cross-cultural religious practices and rituals; great world religions and theologies; spirituality; altered states of consciousness research; Asian, especially Indian religious philosophy and culture; politics; and Sixties politics, culture, movements, and people. As an undergraduate in the early Seventies, my liberal arts studies focused on humanistic psychology at Franklin and Marshall College. I got a degree in humanistic psychology from the University of Colorado at Denver in 1979. I did doctoral work in psychological anthropology at University of California, San Diego. I received an interdisciplinary M.A. — psychology, anthropology, philosophy, history — from Sonoma State University in Prenatal and Perinatal Psychology in 1994.

I have engaged in considerable activism on a number of issues related to peace, justice, and the environment, particularly the problem of nuclear power. Working as a political activist with Oregon Fair Share in the early Eighties, I was one of the score or so involved in the actions that led to ending nuclear plant construction in the entire United States.

For over forty years, beginning in 1972 when I was a senior undergraduate in college, I have been involved both personally and professionally in a comprehensive investigation into the phenomenon of re-experience. Also called reliving, this phenomenon is reported to consist of a full somato-cognitive remembering of previous events in a person's life. Reliving involves experiential but also observable and measurable components, such as brain wave changes, characteristic physiological and neurological changes, and typical observable body movements.

My interest in the phenomenon of reliving began forty-four years ago at Franklin and Marshall College in Lancaster, Pennsylvania. As an undergraduate there I was most inspired by a course in religious studies titled "Religious and Psychological Approaches To Self-Understanding." I was so inspired by the course that I constructed my major around its topic and initially even used the same title for my program's name. This major in "self-understanding" would lead me, in a few years, to a profound interest in and exploration of primal therapy, as presented by Arthur Janov (1970) in his much-publicized book, *The Primal Scream: Primal Therapy: The Cure for Neurosis.*

By 1972, I had completed all but the one final semester for a B.A. That semester was to include the cumulative project — required of such a Special Studies (individually structured) major. However, since my project would focus on primal therapy and one of primal therapy's basic premises is that knowledge cannot really be known except through experience, I could not in good conscience turn in a project describing primal therapy without first experiencing it. Consequently I withdrew from college, for what was supposed to be only a semester, with the intention of "going through" primal therapy and then returning to school to write my cumulative project on it. In those days, the entire process of primal therapy was reputed to take only three to six months.

But a lot was unknown about that modality in those early days. As it turned out, I would not return to school to complete that final project until 1978 — at which point I had five years' experience of primal therapy behind me and was living in Denver, Colorado.

In addition to these experiences, I have amassed a broad array of other experience and training over the years that have contributed to my understanding of re-experience and of this field in general. Besides my two decades and more of primal therapy ... both formally and in "the buddy system" ... I have received training as a primal therapist. I am also a trained rebirther, having explored that modality since 1986. I have been experientially exploring the modality of holotropic breathwork since 1987 and did training with Stanislav and Christina Grof in that technique.

Finally, I have been facilitating people in their journeys into deep inner primal and holotropic states since 1975. I've given individual sessions in all three modalities of primal therapy, rebirthing, and holotropic breathwork. And with my wife, Mary Lynn Adzema, I conducted three day workshops in something we called primal breathwork. I have conducted two-day group workshops in this modality at conferences, which were attended by as many as sixty experiencers at a time.

Thus, I have experience in my own process in these modalities; but in addition I have facilitated for others on many occasions, and at times, it was my main profession — though most of my life I have spent in writing, teaching, and research.

Things I take pride in: all of my writings; any way I've helped clients in therapy; any way I've helped students when I taught at the universities; my websites and blogs, the fact that I was a hippie and a young radical and antiwar activist in the Sixties; the fact that I lived during the incredible Sixties and got to experience and get bitten by the idealism and global visionary bug, which I hold fast, to this day; and the fact that I was the perfect age to understand and experience it — in my late teens and early twenties; the fact that I had the sense and courage to do thorough primal therapy in Denver during the years 1975-1980; my wife, Mary Lynn, and my family.

My main mission in life: Searching for truth in a world of Lies, Liars; wanting to help as we kill the planet, all of us, all our children, grandchildren, and all the planetmates, all the beings, of which God made millions of species, who have lived and had a home on this planet until only lately, the planet-killing half-borns, the species, *Homo sapiens*, evolved, to the extreme detriment of the millions of other planetmates.

Damn good example of why you should get references, *always*, before allowing anyone to move in.